RETIREMENT MANUAL

RETIREMENT MANUAL

A no-nonsense guide to a happy and healthy future

Published in August 2012

A catalogue record for this book is available from the British Library

ISBN 978 0 85733 161 8

Haynes Publishing,
Sparkford, Yeovil, Somerset BA22 7JJ, UK
Tel: +44 (0) 1963 442030
Fax: +44 (0) 1963 440001
E-mail: sales@haynes.co.uk
Website: www.haynes.co.uk

Haynes North America, Inc.,
861 Lawrence Drive, Newbury Park,
California 91320, USA

Printed in the USA by Odcombe Press LP,
1299 Bridgestone Parkway, La Vergne, TN 37086

Photography
Front cover: Masterfile
All other images – Shutterstock and Rex Features (unless credited otherwise)

Author's acknowledgements

My grateful thanks go to all the following who have helped me in various ways with this book. I must single out my daughter, Nicola, who made a major contribution to many parts of the book, although as unelected spokesperson for those listed she has asked me to stress that the errors are all my own work. This I gladly do.

Revd Mark Abrey, Dr Kay Baxter, Bob Charlesworth, Rhonda Charlesworth, Allan Dean-Lewis, Jackie Dean-Lewis, Howard Dent, Dr David Edwards, Richard Eggar, Jane French, Cliff Gaskin, Rob Gaskin, Stuart Guest, Tom Guest, John Jago, Caroline Jeffery, Edgar Jessop, Tim Johnson, Colin Martin, Tony Mason, Mike Moreton, Mike Neville, Roger Neville, Dominic Ostrowski, Gunnar Palm, Sheila Pennington, Bob Rae, Peter Rodwell, Dr Ian Roberts, Graham Robson, Chris Sole, Michael Southcombe, John Sprinzel, John Stanger-Leathes, John Taylor, Dr Nicola Turner, Sarah Turner, Emma Tustin, Rod Waller, Frank Williams, Nigel Yeadon.

Plus all those I have forgotten but will remember the moment the book is published.

Contents

Retirement
Just Ahead

Introduction

Statistics can be shaded to prove anything so I don't intend to saturate the book with them, but these help to set the scene:

- There were 11,600 centenarians in 2009. It is forecast there will be 110,000 by 2035.

- A quarter of today's under-16-year-olds are likely to reach 100.

- In the next 25 years or so the number of those over 65 will double but the number of people working will fall.

Clearly those figures are going to present serious funding issues both in pensions and in health care; too many seem ignorant of what pensions they will receive or how much they will need for a reasonable retirement. We may see an increased move to part-time work as people ease into retirement and as the laws relating to employment of the elderly continue to evolve. So far, increased lifespan has been converted into extra leisure time, but the figures just won't stack up for that to continue. Future generations will have to work longer.

But whatever happens, living longer does not have to mean loneliness or poverty in retirement, especially if you plan ahead. And lots of help is available, as the list of organisations at the back of the book shows, while changing attitudes are helping too, with people now talking openly about dementia and other problems which were once taboo.

And there can be perks in growing old – not just financial ones. When you were very young people may have said you were wonderful for your age; they might start saying the same thing as you grow old, while your joints may become more accurate meteorologists than any weather forecasters. And at least men can relax and finally stop trying to hold their stomachs in, no matter who passes on the beach. Talking of men, throughout the book for 'he' read 'she' too. I just didn't want to cut down more trees to provide the paper for the endless duplication.

Disclaimer time. Although I have survived 20 years of retirement and staggered to my 80th year with all parts still in working order, and although I have invested in property, spoken at more funerals than I care to count, celebrated a golden wedding, and still help run a charity, and although I have consulted widely for the book, I am not a medical or financial expert, so if, for instance, you are planning self-surgery with a Swiss Army knife or intending to accept the share of the 40 million dollars being offered online by your new friend in Nigeria, well, do please get expert advice first.

Finally, in these health and safety conscious times I would like to stress that no pensioners were harmed during the making of this book.

Stuart Turner, 2012

Above: The author, right, with Bernie Ecclestone who has not let encroaching years lessen his influence on Formula One.

MAKING THE MOST OF THE MIDDLE YEARS

Having healthy middle years means that you are more likely to enjoy healthier later years, so this chapter looks at what you should and shouldn't do to maintain a healthy lifestyle, which can be more important than your genes in determining how long and healthily you live.

Healthy eating

I'm not going to insult you by making this yet another diet book; shelves in charity shops already groan under them. You know if you are overweight – a glance in the mirror at the wobbly bits when nude may provide a clue, and you know it's not thyroids but in the brain. 'But I've got heavy bones.' No you haven't, unless a lifetime's devotion to heavy metal music has turned them to lead.

You know that obesity may affect your joints in later life and that controlling your calorie intake affects the speed at which cells age. Avoiding obesity may also reduce the threat of Alzeimer's.

You know, too, that when reading the endless research studies 'proving' the benefits – or otherwise – of this, that and the other foods, that a pinch of salt is recommended. Although not too big a pinch because too much salt is not a Good Thing as it can raise blood pressure and lead to heart attacks and strokes. Nor is over-consumption of sugar wise.

If you have a serious weight problem – and this could be an under- not over- weight issue – see your doctor. In extreme cases he may suggest a gastric band, which reduces the amount you eat before you feel full. You still need to pay attention to diet and exercise when one is fitted, though, and, as with any operation, there can be a risk. Liposuction? Fat removed tends to return within a year and not always in the same or safest places, so this is not the solution to a weight problem. Your GP and your own head will probably tell you that willpower and a diet are the answer.

Tips to keep in mind over diet and weight

● It is much harder to shift fat than it is to avoid putting it on in the first place.

● Yo-yoing up and down the weight scale between umpteen different diets is considered unwise although, as so often the case in the diet field, there is other research suggesting that mice live longer on such diets. But surely you are a man or women, not a mouse. More cheese?

● Barely 10% of dieters succeed in losing weight and then keeping it off, although putting in the effort with more exercise and a better diet may at least give you better health and reduced blood pressure.

● Choose a diet you are likely to stick to, rather than a faddy one which you won't. You need to readjust your overall approach to food.

● Plan your approach to a diet like a military campaign; you'll certainly need military discipline.

Choose a diet you are likely to stick to, rather than a faddy one which you won't. You need to readjust your overall approach to food.

- Use support groups, local or national. What worked for friends may work for you, and it will help having people with whom to discuss things. You can even get personal diet information fed to your mobile phone. Perhaps one will cry 'no' as the burger touches your lips?

- Keep a what-you-ate diary.

- Don't set a crazy target, such as losing a stone in a week. It will probably just pile straight back on.

- It may help to have a target weight which is easy to remember such as 10 stone (or 10 pounds if you are a supermodel, of course).

- Get a good, easy-to-read set of scales and keep them on a firm, level surface. Some scales will speak your weight; perhaps there should be ones that tell you off or just give a hollow laugh when you step on them. Others can link to your computer so that you can keep your friends closely in touch with your diet progress. Whether that's the way to keep your friends is your call of course.

- Weigh yourself once a week – not every hour – in the same state of dress or undress.

- Clock watch … the most likely time to snack or go off a diet is mid-afternoon. But don't clock watch when eating because those who eat quickly are more likely to be overweight than those who don't.

- Beware of just glancing at the calorie count of something like a cake, then only noticing when you've scoffed it all that the figure refers to only a tenth of a slice.

- Be a shade sceptical of foods described as 'light' or 'reduced fat'. Check the labels.

- An apple a day is not just an old wives' tale – enjoying your five portions of fruit and vegetables a day may reduce the risk of heart disease, stroke and some cancers.

Dieting

Assuming you have had the willpower to reduce weight, you may think 'Easy, I can do it anytime', then pile on the pounds again. That is risky because you may find it a lot harder the next time. So how can you keep weight off?

- Reach a weight you feel comfortable with, then buy a skirt or trousers with a non-elasticated waistband and vow always to be able to get into that garment. There are mixed views on whether weight round the waist increases the risk of strokes and heart attacks any more than general obesity does, but it's by far the most noticeable place to carry excess weight and certainly the most rewarding to improve.

- Don't become obsessed about calorie counting, although if you have something as a regular meal look at alternative brands too – one may be 100 calories less than another, yet provide the same sense of enjoyment. Look for salt content as well; some of your favourite pies may surprise you.

- Have breakfast. Rushing out on just a cup of coffee is not a sensible start to a day.

- Shop wearing dark glasses – you may be less seduced by attractive food packaging.

- Don't shop when hungry.

- Consider a time lock for your fridge door and put a photograph on it of you at your fattest.

- Going to a party? Drink some water beforehand so that you don't quench your thirst with wine; you may, of course, have to keep popping to the loo but this may be useful exercise.

- Sit in windows at restaurants because the stream of obese people going by on any inner-city street may act as a powerful appetite depressant.

- Finally, if you order a whooperwhatsitburger with triple fries, remember that specifying a diet cola with it does not turn it into a healthy meal.

Exercise

Regular exercise should be an integral part of your middle years, not least because it can improve co-ordination and muscle strength, which can reduce the risk of falls as you grow older. Exercise also reduces high blood pressure, makes you sleep better and may even ease depression and help you live longer. And it will help you feel sharper and more alert. What's not to like? Some useful tips include:

- Rowing machines? Treadmills? Borrow or at least try one for a spell before buying because your early enthusiasm may flag. If it doesn't, then look online at eBay or Gumtree because countless sheds and garages are cluttered with unused machines.

- Simple things may help. Keep the TV remote control several feet away. Sitting slumped in front of a television can reduce your lifespan, although some programmes may make life seem longer. Get off buses a stop early and walk. Standing rather than sitting on buses and trains – you may have to do this on some services anyway – may burn 70 calories an hour. Use stairs not lifts.

- Any exercise, preferably in the fresh air, can be good – gardening, bowls, swimming (no stress on the joints), squash, riding, tennis, etc. Try hula-hooping with the grandchildren.

Team sports can give an adrenalin buzz, motivating you to keep going with an activity and helping you make friends.

....

- It's never too late to benefit from exercising. The aim should be to raise the heart rate. (I misunderstood my doctor when he told me to do something every day to make me out of breath. I started smoking.)

- Have a medical check before starting an exercise regime especially if, say, you have high blood pressure.

- Don't go mad on an over-ambitious exercise regime. Build up gradually.

- Seek professional advice if you can afford it so that you have a fitness programme tailored to your needs, taking into account your weight and fitness level. If there is a sports club where you work, perhaps develop a routine there that you can carry into retirement.

- Again depending on cost, a personal trainer may help keep you motivated.

- Should you consider joining a health club, check that there is an unambiguous get-out clause because a high number of people stop going after the initial novelty has worn off. Finding a club near your home may help you keep attending in poor weather. Some clubs, especially council-run ones, may offer oldies discounts at off-peak times.

- Allow an hour after eating before exercising.

- An easy routine to remember may help, such as 10 of this or 20 of that every morning and evening.

- Do things you enjoy so that exercise is not seen as a penance.

- Dancing can be useful exercise (whether belly, line or ballroom), but it needs to be energetic, not just slow waltzes.

- The fittest 80 year old I know swears by golf (and swears at it too sometimes) because you move your body, walk several miles, meet people, argue about rules, keep a scorecard, have to remember where all your fellow competitors have lost their golf balls in the rough and so on. And you can enjoy and play

with much better players and still beat them, thanks to the clever handicap system.

- Pilates can improve your health and overall fitness level and Tai Chi helps balance and flexibility – they may not be strenuous, but they can be equal to a brisk walk and may also have psychological benefits. Yoga? It may be a misleading impression, but there can seem to be too much mysticised spiritual rigmarole about it for some tastes. It does help flexibility, though, and enthusiasts swear by it. You will almost certainly find local groups for all these activities.

- Team sports can give an adrenalin buzz, motivating you to keep going with an activity and helping you make friends.

- Good sex is helpful because there is no wear and tear on the joints (unless you are outlandishly adventurous).

- Walking is simple and effective and may be better than spending time in a garage on an exercise machine. But it should be power walking, i.e. brisk. Taking a gentle amble doesn't do a lot of good.

- Running or jogging? Well, every mile you jog adds one minute to your life, apparently, which I think means that at 85 you might spend an additional five months in a nursing home at £3,000 per month. But ask around before you run off. My friends may be unlucky, but those with knee problems in their later years seem to be the ones who used to jog or run half marathons. Not surprising, I suppose, if you think of the pounding the joints may take.

- Whether walking, jogging or running, get the right footwear for the job and, to help your bragging rights later, perhaps wear a pedometer to note how much ground you cover.

- Cycling? Certainly good exercise and joining a cycling club is a really good way of making friends, but on behalf of motorists everywhere can I plead that you wear something bright so that we can see you? And do leave the pavements free for pedestrians.

- Finally, replacing fluids if you perspire is important.

Smoking

As with weight, you don't need me tell you that smoking is stupid and will make you more likely to suffer from lung diseases and die earlier. A male smoker may knock 13 or more years off his life, feel more stressed than non-smokers and, statistics suggest, be more likely to be divorced. Smoking doesn't do the skin a lot of good either, yet you still see young girls puffing away.

As with dieting, the determination to stop has to come from you but the following tips may help:

- Patches and inhalers may double your chance of stopping.

- It will help if you can get friends and relatives to support you.

- Gradual reduction in smoking or cold turkey? The latter would be a lot harsher but perhaps more effective. Whatever works for you.

- When the going gets tough, remind yourself that your body benefits from the moment you quit. After giving up for 10 years, the risk of a heart attack for an ex-smoker would be the same as for a non-smoker. Not a bad incentive for stopping, is it?

- Many people need around five attempts before they give up smoking so don't despair if your first try fails.

- A local NHS Stop Smoking service will be able to help and will increase your chances of stopping.

- It may help to keep a log of your cigarette consumption while trying to stop.

Alcohol

Age is not a reason for abstinence. But it is not a reason for over-consumption either – alcohol puts over a million people a year into hospitals in the UK.

To help you keep consumption under control:

- Know the unit value of your favourite tipple as this may help you stick to the recommended daily units of 3–4 for men (equal to a pint and a half of 4% beer) and 2–3 for women (equal to a 175ml glass of wine).

- Don't forget that alcohol can rapidly add to your calorie intake; with a pint roughly equal to a burger, beer bellies are aptly named.

- Older people are less able to process alcohol than the young (although they may not care).

- Be aware of the effect of alcohol on any medication you take.

Before leaving drinking, do you really need the ever-present water bottle as a fashion accessory? No. The idea that you need six to eight glasses of water a day is an urban myth. But by all means drink water instead of sugary pap.

Above: This calculator from Drinkaware, an independent alcohol awareness charity, shows the alcoholic content of various drinks as well as the number of calories they contain.

Don't be over-ambitious. Having watched an episode of *Casualty* or *Holby City* does not give you a medical qualification.

First aid

- Take steps to prevent you yourself needing first aid by knowing how to lift things properly.

- Consider going to a basic first aid class.

- Should you then come across a road accident, first protect the scene because you won't be able to help anyone if you too become a casualty.

- You fear you will be squeamish? Any sensitivity over the sight of blood is likely to disappear with the pressure of being involved in helping someone.

- Don't be over-ambitious. Having watched an episode of *Casualty* or *Holby City* does not give you a medical qualification.

- Remember FAST (face–arm–speech–time) to help recognise the symptoms of a stroke:

    F can the person smile or is there a facial weakness? Has the side of their eye or mouth dropped?

    A arm weakness. Can the person raise both their arms?

    S speech. Can the person speak clearly and understand what others are saying?

    T time to dial 999 if someone has failed any of the tests so that they can be rushed to a hospital for urgent treatment. Treating strokes as quickly as possible after they occur can greatly reduce the chances of death or permanent disability.

Giving blood

Having considered how to help yourself by following a healthy lifestyle, consider how you can help others, by giving blood. Only 4% of us do so. Just under a pint of blood is taken and, yes, the staff have all heard the Tony Hancock joke about 'a whole armful'. It takes about an hour and is not painful or distressing (which I can confirm as both a donor and a confirmed coward). You will hardly feel a thing, but you may help save a life.

Organ donor card

Some 96% of people would accept a donated organ if they needed one, but only just over a quarter of us have joined the NHS Organ Donor Register. Yet on average three people a day die before they can have a transplant simply because not enough organs are available. It's easy to register. Just go to www.organdonation.nhs.uk or pick up a leaflet at your GP's surgery. There's no age limit – people in their 70s and 80s have become donors and saved lives, and few medical conditions rule you out. You know it makes sense.

CHAPTER 2 Retirement Manual

ALL THE TIME
IN THE WORLD

Draw up a 'bucket list' of things to see or try before you kick the bucket? Or draw up a list of the concerns you have and then determine how to tackle them.

The amount of spare time available to you on retirement may come as a pleasant surprise, but the joy may soon turn to bored disappointment unless you find things to do that give you a reason to get up in the morning. To quote C. S. Lewis:

You are never too old to set another goal or to dream another dream.

Perhaps draw up a 'bucket list' of things to see or try before you kick the bucket? Equally importantly, draw up a list of the concerns you have and then determine how to tackle them.

An interest can keep you stimulated and may help stave off memory problems later – although don't take up something just to stave things off, choose something you enjoy. Almost anything will be healthier than spending hours in front of the TV. The possibilities for pastimes are endless, and I have listed just a few examples.

Writing

You may get stimulus in retirement from books and joining a reading club to make new friends, but if you have had an interesting life or enjoy an absorbing hobby, why not write about it? If you decide to try:

- Don't expect to become a millionaire. But don't underestimate the sheer joy of seeing your masterpiece in print.

- It's not easy, but try to find a publisher before starting. Send them a synopsis showing chapters and an outline of their contents.

- No joy with a publisher? Consider skipping paper and going straight online, or even publishing a printed book yourself. You will see plenty of ads for companies offering help with the process, but do be cautious. Yes, they may tell you your work is a gem (well, they would, wouldn't they?) but be sceptical and do check the small print. Consider doing a batch yourself with a local printer, provided you feel you will be able to distribute

and sell the work. A small financial point: if you are quoted a price for 'run ons' keep in mind that the price for them will only apply if the extras are done at the same time as the original batch.

- Get a friend to read the text and play devil's advocate; this may help make the book more reader-friendly.

- Beware of libel. Don't write a book just to settle old scores!

- Don't dream. A book won't write itself.

- Whether as the subject of a book or just for interest, consider digging into the family tree. There are many groups around, as well as internet sites for help, and there may be immense pride in finding that a great, great relative was a highwayman or courtesan.

Motorsport in Battledress

The story of the Bar-None Motor Cycle Club

Cliff Gaskin

Learn an instrument

Your neighbours may well contribute to that new double glazing you've always wanted, but taking up the challenge of learning to play the piano, banjo or whatever can be really absorbing.

Singing

Mothers sing to babies to soothe them, so it should work for oldies too and joining a choir can be a good way to make friends. At one time, healing chants were actually used instead of pills, but please don't tell the bean counters in the NHS.

Mind games

- Chess or bridge can be mentally stimulating. Neurological research suggests they seem to help stave off dementia, but beware that being bridge partners doesn't damage your marriage.
- Doing a daily crossword, codeword or Sudoku puzzle is not a bad habit to acquire.
- Consider joining a Scrabble club.

Below: Retirement may give you time to produce books on interesting experiences you've had, or about relatives, or to help a local church.

Walking

If you have always been a regular walker perhaps expand this interest by joining a walking club. You will find these will have walks graded in severity, so don't fear that you may have to walk from Land's End to John O'Groats. Well, not in the first week anyway.

Studying

This can be rewarding and research in America has indicated that studying may even help keep blood pressure down. Many local colleges run courses specifically for older people. If you are planning to move to another country consider learning the language, or perhaps study for a degree. If you get combined degrees in Statistics and Applied Code Breaking you may be unique as the only person in your street able to understand tariffs for mobile phone services, energy supplies and rail tickets.

Art

Anyone can draw or paint (well, if monkeys and elephants can paint…). You don't have to dress up, the cost of materials needn't be extortionate, you can do it on your own or join a class, and if you say the result is Art, then it is Art … no need to genuflect before art 'experts'.

Gardening

As well as being useful exercise, gardening gets you out of the house into the fresh air and you can go at your own pace. This perhaps explains why there are long waiting lists in many areas for allotments (there's something very comforting about the lines of slightly decrepit wooden huts on them). And gardening may save you money if you grow your own veg. But if you are new to gardening, make haste a shade slowly – you won't be supplying all the local chip shops with potatoes in your first year. Try a few things before investing too heavily in equipment and time; many producers now offer catalogues with vegetable starter packs.

If you have enough garden, perhaps consider keeping chickens. Get at least three or four to start with as they are quite sociable; the type you acquire depends on whether you want them as ornaments or egg layers. Most pet and farm shops will sell appropriate food for them, and they are low maintenance – you don't have to take them for walks, for example. I would advise against giving them pet names because you may then be more distressed if a fox has one for dinner, or you yourself do with chips and peas.

Finally, there is one great advantage – visit any charity shop and you'll find shelves full of gardening books. The same applies to books if cooking becomes your hobby, but as boiling an egg stretches my expertise let us move on quickly ... to perhaps the most rewarding area of all to occupy a retirement, volunteering.

Volunteering

People have many reasons for volunteering – to do something different, help society, gain skills, meet people, or become an 'insider' – for instance, by helping a theatre or sports team. There are countless opportunities for voluntary work:

- The church. It's not for everyone, but having some internal belief system does seem to have a positive effect on happiness and gives a sense of purpose. Churches will welcome support, especially from those able to help with fundraising or recruitment campaigns because, like many organisations, some churches face declining numbers and an increasing average age.

- Mainstream or local politics, perhaps? Become a councillor if you feel strongly about local matters and want to make a difference to your neighbourhood. But check what power the body you stand for actually has before committing your time, and do think of your blood pressure.

- Many charitable organisations are short of volunteers and you are sure of a welcome. The amount of time you give will be up to you; it could be as little as one hour a week manning a helpline or visiting someone. Perhaps trial something before deciding and don't then over-commit and let people down; don't back out after wasting their money training you.

- Volunteering abroad can be very satisfying, particularly if you are prepared to muck in and get your hands dirty. Do your research carefully first, though, and if possible consult people who have actually done what you are considering. Rip-offs are not unknown, where you may be asked to contribute more than a trip is actually worth. Consider the weather where you are planning to go as well as your personal safety, and do read the small print – is insurance included, for example?

- If you volunteer for something where children are involved, most organisations will sensibly insist that you have a Criminal Records Bureau (CRB) Disclosure undertaken.

As a volunteer this should be free of charge but check with the organisation in advance. There is a Basic Disclosure and a higher level Enhanced Disclosure – the organisation should tell you which is most appropriate and offer explanatory notes to complete what can seem a complicated form. Having a CRB does not mean that people don't trust you. It is a legal requirement and, although the check is primarily to protect children, it can be seen as a degree of protection for yourself, such as in the event of false allegations being made.

Promotion

With so many charities and other organisations fighting for funds, you may find the promotional side of volunteering rewarding. Communication whether by paper, via the internet or on the phone may basically mean preparing a press release. If so, you just need to remember the five Ws: What is happening? Who is involved? When it is happening? Where it is happening? And sometimes the fifth W – Why it is happening, e.g. to protest against a new supermarket.

It is fairly easy, especially these days with email. The problem is that yours won't be the only news item so, in order to get noticed, don't make press releases too long, do make them interesting, avoid jargon, and put in the main information early as journalists may cut from the bottom up.

Newspapers are unlikely to send staff photographers to your event, but they may well use a photograph or two emailed to them (the preferred route) and with clear details of who is involved. You will, of course, remember to get the charity or club logo discreetly in the picture, won't you?

Don't forget local radio – some club spokespeople find themselves approached on other loosely related matters, simply because they've made an effort to build a relationship.

If you volunteer for something where children are involved, organisations will sensibly insist that you have a Criminal Records Bureau (CRB) Disclosure undertaken.

Lobbying

Instead of promoting something you might also become involved in lobbying for or against something, not least perhaps in trying to change attitudes towards ageing. Positive lobbying may be more effective than fulminating on forums or simply moaning that 'something must be done'. Keep in mind:

- Yes, millions sign up to online petitions but the sheer numbers can, in fact, deaden their impact, so don't think local efforts will be wasted.

- Clearly identify the issue and don't cloud it. If lobbying to save the lesser-humped tree frog, don't digress into how concerned you are about the white rhino.

- Identifying your target audience will help you decide how to reach them.

- Be concise. If you've a complicated case to put over, include any minutiae as an attachment.

- Present your case in the best light, but don't lie. If caught your credibility will be holed and your case will sink with it.

- Be wary of over-reacting. If you protest about a bad write-up tucked away on page seven of a local newspaper, your complaint may turn the issue into an unwelcome page one lead.

Public speaking

As part of promoting a charity or organisation, you may find yourself involved in public speaking, as you also might if you have had an interesting life or hobby. Being retired doesn't mean you have to be a retiring type.

- Nerves are perfectly natural. I once had the privilege of sitting next to the great Eric Morecambe at a dinner where we were both speaking and he told me that he believed nerves are due to the fear of failing. I've even heard it said that people fear speaking more than death, but that must be a mild exaggeration otherwise it would mean people at a funeral would rather be in the coffin than standing at the pulpit.

- Think about your audience – Who are they? How many? How old? And what are they expecting from you – information or entertainment?

- Avoid jargon, blue material or swear words. Yes, I know you hear them a lot on TV but, please, not at the sewing circle dinner.

- Remembering your speech? You can, of course, write it out in full and this is the safest way if you are very nervous or have lots of facts to put across. But to stop it sounding stilted, write things to be said, not read – 'it's raining' not 'it is raining'. You could obviously memorise it all, but that's a bit like hard work. 'Bullet points' are perhaps the best option, using key words to remind you of what to say.

- Most important of all, remember nobody gets criticised for speaking too briefly, plenty do for rambling on too long.

- Don't get over-excited at the speaking fees the media sometimes quote as being earned by leading figures. Such figures tend not to trickle down, although you may graduate to being paid something for speaking – at the very least you should be offered expenses. Attending a local chapter of the Professional Speaking Association will give you an opportunity to consult other speakers for advice.

Pets

Keeping a pet can be good therapy, although something of a tie if you are hoping to travel in your retirement. But at least you'll get exercise – if you walk a dog every day you may have walked the equivalent of round the world in its lifetime, which is perhaps why a dog-loving friend advises against buying a dog more energetic than you are. Cats clearly give owners great pleasure, although perhaps not much exercise.

Whatever the pet, there is likely to be a charity prepared to re-home or care for it if you die first.

Holidays

Ignore the friends ribbing you that your retirement is one long holiday and consider taking a break. Wise travel expert friends tell me that we oldies should consider the following if travelling abroad:

- Don't try to cram in too much, such as trying to see all of Australia in a couple of weeks. You can't, no matter how young or fit you are.

- Don't leave it too late to travel. Go while you are fit enough to enjoy the experience and visit the sites.

- Check on facilities for the disabled, if necessary, and seek advice from your doctor about medication. Medical standards may not be the same in other countries. (They may be better in some, of course.)

- Shop around for travel insurance. If you have a particular health issue, charities working in that field may know of helpful insurers.

● Home swaps seem to be a growing trend for holidays. Be clear on what is involved and what is being offered, and advise your home insurers.

● Cruises: check brochure prices against those from agents, be clear what extras there are, and book through an ABTA agent so that you are protected. Cruises seem to attract strongly differing views. Some people feel that instead of travelling on a ship like a floating city, boasting of its multiple cinemas and theatres, you can get the same effect by going to Blackpool, hitting the town, then sleeping on a waterbed. For others they are a hugely popular retirement relaxation, although on some of them the food rather than the scenery seems to be the main attraction, with passengers actually leaving on-board theatres in the middle of entertainers' acts in order to be in pole position when the dining-room doors open. That is perhaps why, in an unguarded moment, one crew member told me that studying passengers on some cruise liners is known as 'on-board whale watching'.

Family and friends

Partners

If you have spent your working life dealing with big wheels in business, it may need quite an adjustment to cope with the smaller wheels on supermarket trolleys. And partners may need adjustment time, too – retirement has been described as twice the husband and half the salary.

Well before 'Retirement Day' partners should make time for an honest discussion about the future, not least to see if they share the same hopes and aims over such things as what to do and where to live. Don't drift into retirement assuming you have identical ideas.

Ideally, have individual interests but also find time for common activities. This will reduce the chance of one partner seeking a new relationship. The internet has made it too easy to contact old, sometimes very old, flames and try to recapture the magic of that faltering first fumble behind the bicycle sheds. I heard of someone who claimed that mathematics was killing his marriage – his wife was putting two and two together.

Other points for partners:

● You may need to guard against friction if both partners are working and then one retires some years before the other because this may unbalance the relationship.

● Keep in mind that poor hearing may adversely affect a partnership. There may be fewer rows after one or both partners have had hearing aids fitted.

● If a marriage breaks down – and divorce among the over 60s is on the increase, apparently – try hard to stay on speaking terms and look into mediation before costly lawsuits.

● A shed as a bolt-hole for one partner may prove an effective marital aid.

● Get a perpetual desk diary for key dates, although the best way always to remember a partner's birthday is to forget it once.

Children

- Keep in with them – they may be the ones choosing your care home.

- Discuss your plans with them.

- Before you rush to move nearer to your children in retirement, are you quite sure that's what they (and, more importantly, any daughter- or son-in-law) really want? You could be marooned with few friends in a strange place, or even a distant country, if things don't work out.

- Don't be too quick with advice, especially to daughters-in-law about rearing children. Just be there if needed.

- While not turning them into gambling addicts, betting children that they won't reach 21 without smoking can be effective. Don't mention the effect of inflation on the sum staked, of course.

Grandchildren

- Discuss do's and don'ts with their parents, i.e. your own children. Know the code words for willies and such, the approach to questions on sex, the policy over watching TV, bedtimes, swearing, and maybe alcohol.

- Try to stop grandchildren over-dosing on computer games as this may damage wrists and fingers.

- Be prepared to become an expert on children's TV programmes and be ready to sing or dance on request.

- Have anti-porn protection in place on any computer. Be alert for any signs of hateful cyber-bullying – a grandchild may decide to confide in you ahead of their parents.

- Remember grandchildren may copy things you do, including any bad eating or vocal habits.

- Encourage them, but don't raise false expectations by over-praise.

- Don't get into 'grannie wars', over-indulging them so that you become the 'preferred' grandparent. Earn their love – don't try to buy it. And try not to favour one grandchild over others.

- Take care with giving piggy-back rides if you've got a bad back. Trampolining? Have a policy of no adults and no booze.

- Know what games they like to play, although their greatest amusement may be caused by your inability to work computer equipment without their help. Of course, you can get your revenge by giving high fives, wearing a baseball cap back to front and dressing young for your age – all these will have grandchildren cringing with embarrassment. If you really want them to behave, the ultimate deterrent will be to threaten to dance. In front of their friends.

- Listen to their views and encourage debate. But make 'no' mean 'no', although don't over-use the word.

- Learn diplomacy. For example, if you have a cake and two grandchildren to share it, let one cut the cake and then the other have first choice of the pieces.

- Don't bad mouth parents in front of children, especially if they have split up, and try not to let kids become pawns in marital disputes – not an uncommon risk now that 1 in 4 children live with one parent rather than two.

- Grandfathers may get suspicious looks when they first appear at school gates. A parent should go along the first time to make introductions. Some schools incidentally hold grandparent days, possibly on the assumption that they may be the ones paying some of the fees.

- With over 14 million grandparents in the UK, it is hardly surprising that there are websites to help. There is also a charity, the Grandparents' Association, to assist those who have lost or are losing contact with their grandchildren, or are caring for them on a full-time basis. With around half of marriages ending in divorce (as do some three-quarters of second marriages), grandparents doing the parenting is common.

Friends

New pastimes and hobbies will help you make new friends, while if you want to start a new relationship there are plenty of newspaper and magazine ads, as well as online dating sites, including some especially for the over 60s.

The internet is fast and easy ... but it is also too easy to lie online and even invent a totally false identity, so if you decide to meet up with someone, consider the risks. Let a friend know where you are going; meet in a public place, in daylight – perhaps where you can beat a hasty retreat if the man who claimed to be 'tall, dark and handsome' turns out to be short, fat and then some.

MONEY
MATTERS

There is no shortage of scare stories about the poverty trap facing people living longer and with inadequate savings or pensions. It is estimated that around a third of us have a casual approach to our long-term financial health and, as a result, buy things we can't really afford and probably don't need anyway.

The wealthier suffer from less depression and have a better quality of life, as well as enjoying better food, although the latter could simply lead to them becoming fatter and more florid. Wealth doesn't necessarily bring happiness, because small things can then lose their meaning, but it is miserable to be really poor and it can directly affect your health, not least by loss of sleep over money matters.

Proper attention to money management can help by highlighting when you should be seeking help – and for money matters, just as for health ones, you should seek professional help when necessary. Have you been in the same financial routine for years? That may be fine, but with retirement is it perhaps time to take stock and maybe do better?

General tips

- Keep a list of any assets whether in savings accounts, Premium Bonds or tangibles like jewellery, your house and so on. Give a copy to a trusted friend or in a sealed envelope to your solicitor, assuming you have made a Will (and you really should). That may all be obvious, but you still hear of relatives finding things squirrelled away in odd places by the deceased. If nothing else, such a list will act as a prompt to having adequate insurance.

- Keep records – letters, invoices and so on – and if keeping records on a computer, have back-up. Don't leave financial papers where they could easily become a burglar's shopping list. And use a shredder before you finally dispose of paperwork.

- Keep a diary of such things as when policies are due for renewal, the MoT is due on the car and so on. And use the diary to note when, for example, tradesmen have been contacted or have promised to do a specific job. Such information will help should you get into a dispute with someone. Note in the diary cut-off dates to cancel things like special offers – many suppliers rely on your inertia to do nothing so that, for instance, a bargain few issues of a magazine can become an unwanted long-term commitment.

- Try to do a regular cash-flow forecast. This may perhaps be asking a lot of many people, but it should at least encourage them to 'think financial'. You can get easy-to-use computer programmes which prompt you with key questions and which mean you don't have to keep adding and subtracting, but a simple notebook and a pocket calculator may suffice. You just need some way of forecasting, and then recording, your likely income and expenditure.

- Try to update the forecast every month. Use averages, if necessary, to forecast the figures, but on no account be over-optimistic. Allow for inflation, allow for contingencies, and under 'income' include only what you are sure of receiving. Include any one-off major items like holidays; doing so may help you save with them in mind.

- Check your figures against any bank statements, and if you can't understand a transaction then query it. Identity theft is quite a threat and if you don't make regular checks you will not know until it's too late.

- Do longer-term forecasts, too – and if you see trouble looming, don't ignore things or delay tackling a problem. Bad news won't get any better if you tuck letters in red ink under a cushion. Remember that financial organisations may be more ready to help if consulted early rather than at the last minute.

- Prioritise your bills and remember that the most vociferous creditors won't necessarily be the most important ones. If someone becomes over-threatening, tell them you will be contacting the police or the trading standards office to complain about illegal harassment.

Check your figures against any bank statements, and if you can't understand a transaction then query it. Identity theft is quite a threat so make regular checks.

- If your forecast shows trouble ahead, several organisations like the Citizens Advice Bureau may be able to help you plan your way forward; see under 'Further information' at the end of the book. You may be able to get help from a charity connected with a previous job you had. Seek such help before overloading a credit card or rushing to a moneylender. However tough things get, do not touch logbook or pay day loans with a barge pole. Not even a disinfected one.

Banking

Once upon a time bankers were regarded with awe, but after their appalling press in recent times they are now far more open to scrutiny. This is a Good Thing. But we still need them.

Around one-third of people are unhappy with their present bank because of things like lack of transparency and poor service. Yet inertia stops people changing.

If you want to switch accounts – whether because you are moving on retirement, or for better service, or to spread your accounts to stay under the current firewall limit if a bank goes bust or, touch wood, for better rates either with a bank or building society – then your present provider must help you do this, not place obstacles in your way. In fact, there may be switching teams in place to help the process.

Banks like current account holders because it gives them a chance to sell their customers other financial products. You may find it convenient to have all your money eggs in one basket, but you don't have to use the same provider for all financial needs – and you could be losing out by doing so.

Only keep what you need in your current account. It pays no interest and if identity theft hits you, the less you have in, the less there will be to steal. Find a few payers of interest that meet your needs, but don't make life too complicated by having too many accounts.

Choose the bank or building society you want to move your money to, fill in their forms and produce the necessary ID, which will include proof of address. You will need to contact those who pay money, such as a pension, into your account and you also need to remember that most problems occur over direct debits, so monitor these carefully.

Many believe free banking will slowly disappear (although new banks may use free accounts as a marketing tool to entice new customers) so in the future, rather than searching for somewhere paying the most interest, you may be seeking somewhere charging you the least. Guarantee cards have already been axed so that your bank no longer guarantees a payment, although this does not mean you cannot use cheques, which seem likely to be around for a while yet. Many places, however, will no longer accept them, but charities are likely to fight for cheques because the majority of their gifts come in that form.

It may, in fact, be as easy to pay by debit card (although charges are likely to apply abroad) or direct debit, a simple way to cope with regular bills, provided you know you will have cash in the account when they fall due. Be cautious, though, over special offers that involve paying by direct debit – check the small print about how to cancel.

And, of course, if you bank online you can do so 24/365. Scared? You don't need to be, because most banks commit to refund you if you are a victim of fraud when banking with them in this way, provided you have followed their guidelines.

Which account you choose depends on what sort of a customer you are likely to be, for instance whether you are likely to go into the red or not. Banks will charge you a very high fee for what it calls an 'unauthorised overdraft'. On the other hand, some institutions may well offer a facility of going, say, £100 overdrawn as part of a deal when negotiating an account.

There may be rewards if you switch to a fee-paying account. Special deals are often linked to some accounts – like travel insurance – but shop around and look long term. Consider how suitable the account will be if a special deal lapses.

'Would you mind if some students watch while we refuse to lend you any money?'

Plastic

- If you know you have no willpower, don't take cards with you when shopping.

- Store cards? Watch the rates, which can be very high.

- Don't use plastic for borrowing – pay debts off in full and on time; pay off high interest ones first.

- Multiple cards? Well, for some people a wallet bulging with cards is seen as a status symbol. But you may find you could do just as well with only one or two – and it would be a whole lot easier to remember the PIN numbers.

- Special deals? Zero percentage credit card deals get publicity via best-buy tables, but do look longer term. What happens when the deal ends? (And note that any special deals are likely to stop if you become overdrawn.)

- Beware of the high fees sometimes charged if you pay by credit card. Check first, as debit cards may be cheaper in some cases.

- To avoid fraud with credit cards, be sure your card company has your up-to-date contact details so that it can get hold of you if there is a problem. Most card companies will cancel all cards with just one call.

- If you're going abroad for that promised trip to celebrate retirement, check the small print over foreign charges. Some credit cards don't charge for overseas usage, while with others the charges can be very high. If there is the option to pay a local bill in sterling or local currency, opt for the local currency because instead of getting the best exchange rate from your card provider, you may get a rate applied by the sales outlet which will, of course, be in their favour not yours.

- Tell your credit card company holder where you are going so that it is not surprised by payments you make in Patagonia. And always have the card company's emergency phone number with you in case of a problem.

- Consider a pre-pay travel card. You can load cash on to them online, or over the phone, or in branches. The card can then be used abroad at hole-in-the-wall machines and in shops and cafes, etc. The benefit is that there is no credit facility, so if a card is stolen it can't be used to raid your bank account. You will, however, pay a redemption fee if you want unspent cash back from such a card.

- Although retirement may give you plenty of time to explore the currency options, you can, of course, avoid much of the hassle by buying foreign currency at home and then using a money belt. This means no holiday time is wasted queuing to change money and it is not easy for pickpockets to access your cash. Mind you, if they do steal your belt it may not be easy to chase them with a skirt or trousers round your ankles.

Pensions

This is a vitally important area for most people, yet less than half of us plan for the future. The majority have little idea of what they will have to live on when they retire and are simply not saving enough, perhaps because they are assuming that their home will fund their retirement – which could be a dangerous presumption – or maybe because of an over-optimistic belief that 'it won't happen to me'.

Retirement is lasting longer, with people having almost twice the years to look forward on retirement as they had 50 years ago, which makes planning even more important.

Under government plans the state pension age will go up to 66 for both men and women by 2020 and to 68 by 2046; this will be done on a sliding scale depending on when you were born. You can, of course, choose to stop work before the stipulated age but you won't receive the state pension before that time. A default retirement age is now illegal, unless your employer can objectively justify it as a 'proportionate means of achieving a legitimate aim'. If you are compulsorily retired you may be able to bring a claim for age discrimination and unfair dismissal.

Beware of the high fees sometimes charged if you pay by credit card. Check first, as debit cards may be cheaper in some cases.

State pensions are not means tested. A lavish private pension plan will not affect your state pension – other than that you will have to pay more income tax.

Many people believe that, despite the outraged reaction to even minor increases in the pensionable age, the figure will have to rise further and faster in future years because there will be too few younger people earning per person retired, so the sums just won't add up. If we are all going to have to work into our 80s, then maybe the key to a happy life will be to find a job you enjoy.

It doesn't help that forecasts about pensions are often wrong, not least because of stock market turmoil, which may be partly why over half of pension schemes are believed to be in deficit. In the long term, inflation can wreak real havoc, while insurance companies can only forecast using government formulae which may bear little relation to reality.

With that cheerful preamble out of the way, consider what pension/s you can look forward to and whether it/they will be sufficient for your later years. Ideally, do this review far enough ahead of your retirement date for there to be time to make improvements if necessary.

- First, of course, there should be a state pension which you will receive on whatever date is the state retirement age at the time of your retirement. If you go to the government's website (www.direct.gov.uk/ betterfuture) you can find an estimate of how much basic state pension you may have built up, as well as a forecast of how much you may need to live on.

- State pensions are not means tested. A lavish private pension plan will not affect your state pension – other than that you will have to pay more income tax, of course.

- Be clear what type of company or private pension you have, if any. Is it geared to the Consumer Prices Index (CPI) which, for instance, does not include housing costs? Or is it linked to the Retail Prices Index (RPI)? A CPI pension is linked to a rise in *consumer* not retail prices, and may leave people significantly worse off. The younger you are, the worse the impact because there will be more years for the difference between RPI and CPI to affect your pension.

- Final salary schemes have been, or are being, closed because they are too expensive. Pensions are now likely to be based on a proportion of your average salary over your career rather than as a proportion of your final salary. This may be particularly tough if you had a hefty salary hike over your last few years in work.

- Most personal and company pension schemes are run on 'money' purchase lines – your contributions are invested in the stock market and your pension then depends on market performance. Your pension will be governed by how much you put in, how long it's been invested and how the investment performs.

'...and this is the day room. Of course everyone's out at work at the moment'

It has been suggested that 25 year olds should be saving 15% of their annual income to be sure of a comfortable retirement.

- Review the state pension along with your company pension and any personal ones you have taken out. Add in any other income you can rely on, say from investments or maybe an expected inheritance (although don't forget that something anticipated from an ageing relative may have to go on their care costs instead).

- It has been suggested that 25 year olds should be saving 15% of their annual income to be sure of a comfortable retirement, while 40 year olds who have not saved should start putting away up to a quarter of their income – although the percentages may depend on what individuals consider enough for a 'comfortable' retirement.

- If your calculations indicate that things may get tight on retirement, look at paying more into your company pension pot via an AVC (Additional Voluntary Contribution scheme). If there is no free-standing AVC scheme, then consider saving into a personal or stakeholder pension. It may be worth taking out another pension via a fee-based independent financial adviser (IFA) rather than adding to your existing one, if this does not provide the diversification of risks and investment with which you feel comfortable.

- The maximum annual sum that can be paid into a pension scheme and qualify for tax relief is currently £50,000, regardless of how much you earn. Saving any more than this in a pension will not be tax efficient. In return for tax relief, you are not allowed to touch your pension pot until you are 55.

- It is common nowadays for people to have more than one pension as lifetime work with just one employer is no longer the norm. At one time you could expect a gold watch when you retired; now you may be lucky if a director pops round and shouts the time through your letterbox.

- If you have several pensions, consider putting them into one pot because one large annuity may be better than several smaller ones, and life may be simpler with just one income source, although check carefully before switching as there can be risks and charges may be high.

- If you retire abroad, you can move UK funds to an overseas pension fund which may have some benefits.

- A Self Invested Personal Pension (SIPP) gives you the freedom to manage and choose your own investments, making the decisions yourself, but SIPPs are really only for funds of, say, £150k upwards and only for those with financial know-how and inclination. Note that you can't use one to invest in residential property.

- On retirement you will have the option of taking 25% of your pension as a lump sum. You might consider doing this if, say, you wanted to invest in property. The benefit is that the lump sum will be tax free, whereas the pension will of course be taxable. For higher-rate tax payers, lump sums can be taken in instalments, to be used as income.

- An annuity means using pension fund capital to buy a pension income annuity. It is worth comparing companies when you have a personal pension, and not necessarily going along with the original insurer for your annuity, for example you may have saved with Company X but Company Y may be doing a better deal Also, you don't have to take out an annuity the instant you retire – you can enter into drawdown where the fund remains invested and an income is drawn from it. This means the funds are part of your estate so if you die they can be left to others; buy an annuity and die and it's goodbye to the funds.

- When you retire, be careful to keep all documents and make a note of anything said or promised at the time. The paperwork may not be easy to follow – it may be even less so in a few years' time when memories have faded. Keeping notes may help if there are disputes later.

- You may need to keep a sharp eye on your pension scheme if new owners take over the company for which you work or worked. Various nefarious schemes may be cooked up by new owners to avoid any obligation to maintain pensions. If a company goes belly up, or avoids its obligations, then a company scheme may be moved under the umbrella of the PPF (the government's Pension Protection Fund), but the result may be reduced pensions. This risk is just one reason why you should strongly support any monitoring of pensions done by any employee/retiree organisations. These can be good watchdogs, alerting pensioners if, say, companies appoint directors as trustees of their pension schemes … they are hardly likely to be impartial negotiators.

- Don't be one of the 50% who don't plan for the future. Instead save, review regularly, and perhaps diversify into ISAs and other funds to give more flexibility. Ensure your pension funds perform and that you review the risks of the funds that you invest in to make sure that they are aligned to your attitude to risk. Incidentally, exactly the same advice applies to the self-employed.

- Finally, remember that pension rules and regulations can change and your personal circumstances will govern what is best for you. If in doubt, seek professional help. This is not a DIY area.

Money making

Making money doesn't have to stop on retirement. You may decide to start that business you have always dreamt about, although the plethora of petty rules you can face might seem designed to deter initiative. Other possibilities include:

- Part-time work, perhaps where you were once employed. Companies trying to reduce their headcount often increase the number of consultants used at the same time.

- Earning via the black economy? No comment.

- Feeling fit and healthy? Then copy a friend of mine and bet that you'll reach 100. His winnings paid for a splendid party.

- Take in a lodger or do a short let while you travel. Tell your insurers about this, as well as your landlord if you yourself are renting.

- If you live near a sports venue holding major events, charge for car parking in your drive or camping on your back lawn. You can allow someone to use your garden for 28 days a year without planning permission – although the neighbours may, of course, have a view about it.

- Car boot sales can be fun and profitable, and will at least help you to clear out clutter, perhaps before you move on retirement. Visit a few to get the feel of them before selling anything yourself. If you're unsure of the value of something there are several online sites to guide you. Also, keep an eye open for auctioneers running valuation days for charities at a pound or two per item. Remember, you can always drop a price, rarely raise one. Collect strong boxes so that it is easy to carry stuff around and present it so it looks its best. Take food and drink with you. And some change. It helps to have someone with you to cover for loo breaks and to guard against theft. Yes, this does happen. Assume it will be wet and cold.

- House sitting, DIY or gardening can all yield a small income.

- Dog walking. You will get exercise at the same time. Have public liability insurance in case a dog in your charge attacks someone.

- eBay trading is an activity that has grown amazingly in recent years. It is easy to do and you can trade even if you are housebound. And it's not just for trading, of course – you can use it to find additions to something you collect or simply to de-clutter.

Dog walking. You will get exercise at the same time. Have public liability insurance in case a dog in your charge attacks someone.

Buying on eBay

- Have a good search thorough various categories before committing yourself – if you want something for a particular car, for example, search by make, model and any other permutation you can think of.

- Make sure that what you are planning on bidding for is really the right thing (if it has a particular application) by asking the seller suitable questions – if you don't receive the answer you want, don't bid. Genuine sellers will be keen to answer questions and provide more information and possibly pictures.

- Check out your vendor: he/she has a feedback rating in brackets after his/her (eBay) name which is a good guide to performance, and you can view their feedback by clicking on the number.

- A genuine seller will always have good quality pictures – avoid bidding on items that have blurred or indistinct images or you may get a surprise when the items arrive.

- Once you've done your homework and decided it's worth a bid (or two), set yourself a limit; it's easy to be carried away and end up paying over the odds.

- Keep an eye on the bidding history for your chosen item as it may well give a clue to the amount of interest in it – check the dates and times of bids.

- Use Paypal if you can to pay for buying items – it works like a credit card with all the same type of protection. If you have a problem with a purchase, e.g. it doesn't arrive, then Paypal will refund your money and take it up with the seller. It's worth making sure that the postage service used for a valuable item is suitable because a tracking number gives great peace of mind.

*'I've been shopping all day
– my fingers are killing me.'*

- Lastly on buying, if you are worried about getting carried away in an auction or can't 'be there' at the end, then use an auction sniping service, of which there are several. A snipe is basically a computer programme that can be pre-programmed to do your work for you; all you have to do is tell it which item, how much to bid to, and how long before the auction ends you'd like it to operate. You pay a very small percentage of the item cost in exchange for the service, but it does fulfil one major need if nothing else: you don't get sucked into a battle for an item, you merely decide beforehand how much you want to spend. These services only bid enough to win the item at the next bid increment, not necessarily up to your maximum, so you won't pay more than necessary.

Keep an eye on the bidding history for your chosen item as it may well give a clue to the amount of interest in it – check the dates and times of bids.

Selling on eBay

- Do your market research first – try to find what your item might fetch, so that you can set a realistic starting price. On a collectable item you can easily risk a low start, but with an item that has a high value or a limited market you might want to set a reserve. It's easier to do it right in the first place than find out later you could have done it better.

- eBay is so big that there are hundreds of categories for listing things in, so do your best to find the most appropriate one for your item.

- Take the best picture you can of your items so that everyone can see exactly what they're bidding for.

- Make your description as accurate as you can. Tell it like it is – if there's a scratch/chip/crack, then mention it. And if you have taken good pictures which reflect the item, and you are honest about the odd fault, then it won't put bidders off.

- Decide how far afield you are prepared to post items; some vendors don't mind sending items all over the world, others won't. It's important to state where you stand on this before you list items as it may have a big impact on who 'looks' at your items. If you don't have time for customs labels and weighing for different countries then don't offer the service.

- If you are selling something which has a part number, list that number even if you aren't sure what it fits – there are plenty of others out there who will know, and they may let you in on the information because they can. Then you can make an alteration to the listing while it's 'live'.

- You may receive questions about the item you're selling. Some will be asking obvious things like postage costs, or have you got a green one rather than the red; you can choose to show questions and answers on the listing, so answer with as much extra information as you can.

- Some members may want you to end your auction early, and offer money to this end. Be very careful because, apart from being a little outside eBay's operating policy, and therefore not covered by any of its safety measures, it generally means that your item is very desirable. Leaving the auction to run full distance may well attract plenty of bidders.

- Last, and most importantly, when you have received and cleared payment for your item, make sure you post it when you say you're going to, and package the item properly. If you want to receive good feedback, make the effort to provide a good service – it will be reflected in what people say about you, then when others check you out before bidding next time, they'll see what a fine and honest person you are.

Perhaps that was rather a lot of information about eBay, but I make no apologies because it really is remarkable, and ideal for retirement because it is not age related. It may even be that a hobby could become a cottage industry. Those toys you made for your grandchildren, for instance – there may well be lots of people who would pay for such individuality. You could be a mere click away from an extra income.

If trading on eBay works works for you – and there's no reason why it shouldn't – you may wish you'd retired earlier in order to become involved.

'The good news is we met payroll. The bad news is
I sold that outfit you're wearing on eBay to do so.'

Saving money

One important way to save money is to take advantage of the many benefits available as you retire and grow old, including:

- State pension.
- Zero prescription charges.
- Free TV licence, or concessions.
- Free or discounted bus passes, hence the term 'twirlies' for those of us asking if we are 'too early' to use such passes.
- Senior railcards.
- Concessions on admission tickets for theatres, exhibitions, etc.
- Discounts on sports facilities, especially if you are an off-peak user.
- Discounted days for pensioners at hairdressers, DIY stores and garden centres and the like (and how flattering to be asked for proof of age).
- Look out for 'pensioners' portions' where for instance you may get a discount at your local chippy or pub for a slightly smaller portion. Resist the urge to reminisce about how much better chips tasted when eaten out of newspapers.
- Bereavement allowance.
- Winter fuel payments.
- Disability allowances.
- Carers' allowances.
- A benefit may be available if you have very poor vision.

And there may be other benefits available to you. Don't be too proud or neglectful to *take* what is on offer. Studies regularly show that many people fail to do so, which is crazy. If you are being means tested for anything it will probably be assumed that you have received whatever is available, whether you have or not. And a further reason for claiming such things is that if people don't then they may be discontinued in future years.

As well as various grants and concessions, you can also save by not wasting money. Online comparison sites are available for almost everything – car and house insurance, hotel bookings, travel, energy supplies and so on. Don't rush to click 'buy', however. Like some travel guidebooks, a number of sites only include companies that pay them, while some perfectly reputable companies refuse to allow their products to be shown on comparison sites.

Booking sites often come up first on internet search engines – for hotels, for instance – but you may get a better deal direct with a hotel, which may be listed on a later 'page'.

Be sure about what you are getting. To appear as best buys, some products may be stripped down to bare essentials, or you may be getting an illustrative quote based on general, rather than your specific, needs. Comparison sites may also lead to you getting cold-called.

Shopping

- Consider group buying with neighbours. Even synchronising central heating oil top-ups can produce savings.

- Oldies should not shop when tired as their judgement may be impaired.

- Make a shopping list and stick to it. The fact that essentials are stocked at the back of shops does not mean that it is compulsory to fill your basket with other items en route.

- Blind comparison taste some of the food you eat most regularly. 'Own brands' can be good value – and if you can't tell the difference between an expensive product and a cheaper version there can be a useful ongoing saving.

If you still pay prescription charges, check if buying the same product would actually be cheaper than paying the charge.

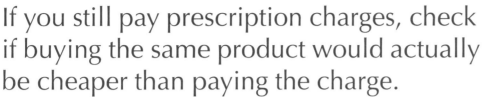

- Learn to resist the words 'just' and 'only' when applied to the price of something. And don't hyperventilate with excitement at seeing 'BOGOF' (buy one, get one free) and '3 for 2' offers.

- Loyalty cards? Yes, but only if you are going to buy the product anyway.

- If you still pay prescription charges, check if buying the same product would actually be cheaper than paying the charge.

- Eco this or eco that does not mean something is a bargain; it may even be more expensive.

- *Which?* magazine can be a great help when buying. See www.which.co.uk

Energy

- All energy companies sign you up for a contract. If you do not give the correct notice you may be rolled over to a contract higher than the advertised rate, so check the relevant date and put it in a diary. And beware of fees if you leave an energy tariff deal early. You really need a crystal ball to forecast when to sign up for energy deals and what will happen in a year or two.

- Switch off unnecessary lights, don't fill a kettle for just one cup of tea (although always cover the element, of course), draw curtains in an unused room to keep the heat in, fit draught excluders and have ample loft insulation … all obvious? Of course, but forgetting such things can add up.

- Don't overcharge devices like laptops and mobile phones. It just adds to your electricity bill and can reduce the life of the batteries.

Watch check-in baggage fees. If you are only going to lie on a beach you may be able to travel with just hand baggage and avoid these fees altogether.

Travel

- Avoid school holiday times, when the prices go up. One advantage of retirement is that you may be able to choose when to go on holiday.

- Watch check-in baggage fees. If you are only going to lie on a beach you may be able to travel with just hand baggage and avoid these fees altogether.

Mobile phone contracts

- Ofcom rules mean that firms have to switch numbers within one working day.

- Beware of pushy deals – 'free' upgrades may be anything but. And as for 'free' minutes, will you really use them all?

- If you are you permanently wedded to your mobile, can you save money by scrapping your landline?

More simple tips for saving money

Other thoughts, many of them minor but which added together can result in a useful saving, include:

- Taking advantage of discounts for prompt payment. Paying promptly can also result in helpful goodwill.

- Check that you have no direct debits or standing orders which you no longer need. Cancel them immediately.

- Plan ahead so that you can use second not first class stamps all the time.

- Read newspapers in libraries or online (if free access), or swap papers and magazines with neighbours.

- Get dripping taps fixed.

- Many of us are vulnerable when it comes to matters like boiler repairs and may be charged for work not done. Word of mouth in finding someone may be better than viewing any ads or slick websites. Check that repair people are members of recognised trade bodies.

- Take advantage of special membership deals such as for the National Trust and CAMRA. These will give cheaper access to attractive properties and gardens, or discounts at some pubs, and you will be supporting two worthwhile organisations in the process.

- Financial columnists in newspapers are worth taking note of, as are consumer programmes on TV. Making it obvious on any letters that you have sent copies to such outlets, as well as MPs and any official complaints channels, may help you to get a recalcitrant supplier's attention.

Scams

- One important way of saving money is to avoid losing it to fraudsters. Such people may target you via an innocent-sounding and friendly phone call saying that you have a virus on your computer. If you respond, they may con you into revealing credit card or other details. Very bright people have fallen for such calls, so great care is advised!

- Fraudsters are even more active online. Their activities may range from homework scams to people being conned into becoming middlemen selling things on eBay when no actual goods exist. You receive an email saying you are due a tax refund? Delete it, because it will not be from the tax authorities. And a special deal is on offer from someone needing help in accessing millions? Again – no.

- Buying tickets online? There may be hysteria at the time of a major sporting event, which can lead to scam sites. Check that there is a landline, not just a mobile number, and if there is a post code then Google to see the premises

and if there is just a shed … forget it. If a friend lives near an alleged vendor, get them to call in person.

- If you still need to buy online then do so from known, reputable sites; perhaps request a photograph which also shows a copy of that day's newspaper.

- When it comes to creating passwords, they should be at least eight characters long and made up of upper and lower case letters, numbers and symbols to ensure good protection. If you don't want to choose a random selection of characters, convert a memorable word. For example, the word 'password' might become p&55W0rd – substituting & for 'a', the number five for every occurrence of the letter 's' and zero (0) for 'o' – but now I have mentioned that, make sure you use something different.

- Although you shouldn't really keep a written record of which user names and passwords to use with each site, a lot of people do. If you decide to do so, at least keep the record in a very safe place. Remember, if you do forget a password, most online retailers will email the details to you, but once they have done that it is advisable to change that password for a new one.

- Use credit cards rather than debit cards for making online purchases. That way, if someone manages to get hold of your details they may be able to make purchases, but they won't be able to empty your current account.

- If you have more than one credit card, it is worth using one card solely for making purchases online. You can then quickly spot any spurious purchases and check that the goods you have ordered online have been delivered.

All rather over-cautious and you may lose a chance to buy a bargain? Maybe, but the fraud out there is massive. It is surely better to be careful than to be conned.

Buying tickets online? There may be hysteria at the time of a major sporting event, which can lead to scam sites.

Motoring costs

- This is an area where word of mouth is helpful because many motorists don't know the difference between a big end and a Big Mac. As with other technical things, like televisions, they are in the hands of the service provider.

- If a garage spouts jargon, ask what they mean. And yes, women may still find themselves patronised.

- Avoid speeding points. They will increase your insurance premiums.

- Keep in mind that short journeys are less economical because cold engines are less efficient. Perhaps use your free travel pass, or walk if possible instead?

- Keep tyres at the right pressure and compare prices if you need new tyres. The irritation and inconvenience caused by a puncture may lead you to rush to the first place you see without considering cost. Online prices may be lower than 'call in' ones. Be sure quotes include balancing and, not least, getting rid of your old tyres. Resist any pressure to fit four new tyres when perhaps you only need two.

- You may find local car clubs organising economy runs. Give one a try – you won't need racing overalls, and seeing how you compare with others in the same model could perhaps alert you to improvements that could be made. Some events issue results in pence per mile, which means that you can directly compare diesel and petrol.

- Try an experiment. Fill your car's fuel tank until the pump clicks. Drive as you normally do for a few days, then fill again until the same pump clicks. Then calculate the mpg and pence per mile you've done. Now drive more gently, avoiding violent acceleration or braking, then fill the tank again until the pump clicks. Repeat the mpg and pence per mile sums and compare them with the previous ones. You may well find that you have saved several pence per mile. Now calculate that saving over your average year's motoring. Bingo!

Diesel v. petrol? Well, modern diesels are not the clatterers of our youth, but calculations vary year by year as to which is the most economical.

- Keep in mind that driving at 70mph uses 9% more fuel than going at 60mph. Driving more slowly means you will make substantial savings and you probably won't even take much longer over your journeys. You will also spend less time scraping flies off your windscreen, although you may have to scrape the odd oddity in a white van off your boot.

- Clear out junk from the car. Heavy rubber car mats? Try lighter carpet offcuts instead.

- Not using that roof rack or box? Remove it to reduce drag and improve fuel consumption.

- If you are just pottering about locally, don't run the car with the weight of a full tank all the time (although keep in mind the hassle should you run out). You may feel less affected by fuel price rises if you always top up with, say, £20 worth at a time – it's a state of mind!

- Check directions before setting off anywhere so that you know exactly where you are going. Driving round in circles trying to find somewhere is not economical. Time for a satnav, perhaps?

- Black boxes are available so that you can tune a car for economy not performance, and the savings may soon pay for such gadgets. But not all manufacturers approve of their use – and do tell your insurers if you fit one.

- Don't necessarily 'buy the badge' – perhaps blind tests cars as you might wines.

- Perhaps buy a car in a weird colour. The price is likely to be lower and at least you should be able to find it in car parks. Whether this balances the social ostracism and the lower trade-in figure when you sell is your call.

- Diesel v. petrol? Well, modern diesels are not the clatterers of our youth, but calculations vary year by year as to which is the most economical.

- Considering switching to a motorcycle? Perhaps not … but if you do, remember that your reactions may not be quite what they were when you were younger, so be cautious about doing wheelies to impress the Darby and Joan Club.

Mortgages

For someone who is close to retirement and has an existing mortgage, the best thing to do will depend on whether their income in retirement will be sufficient to cover their mortgage payments. Basically, lenders have little forgiveness for those who don't pay, whether young or old. Unless the house can be sold and a smaller property purchased using the remaining equity after clearing the mortgage, then there may be no other option but to plod on with the existing arrangement.

Someone aged 60 should be able to get a mortgage from a few lenders, either for a first home (if, say, they had always rented or been in a company house), or even for a second home or for a property for grandchildren to use while at university.

For a first home, as long as the individual's job role allows them to work past the perceived retirement age, some institutions will lend up to the age of 75 and take all the income up to this point into account in their calculations, although when an individual passes 60 or 65 years most lenders will only take pension and other forms of retirement income into account. It's important to note that a bank offering this service would probably have an issue with believing someone who is in a physically demanding job will be able to work past the normal retirement age. Office and desk-based jobs will sit better with them.

For a second home, a buy-to-let mortgage would be possible with a few lenders; some will lend up to 90 years of age and at least one has no age limit at all. A pensionable income of some description will still be required by these lenders, but the amount they will lend is based on the potential return of the rental property, not the level of the individual's actual income.

For a residential mortgage (buying a home to live in) most residential lenders will stop at a maximum

It's a tough market out there. Any stains on your financial record, such as difficulty with a credit card, could adversely affect your chances of getting a mortgage.

age of 70 or 75 (some even at 60), although of course at such ages you would only have a short term on a loan, which could make the repayments very expensive.

It has been known for someone to buy a property on a buy-to-let basis (giving a much longer term) and then decide to move in themselves. As long as the lender is getting their money each month they will probably be happy (although I would never suggest that anyone does such a thing, of course).

The deposit required should not increase with age, although sometimes with the smaller building societies, if the underwriter is uneasy with signing off a case, then an increase in deposit, thus reducing the lender's exposure, might swing a deal. This kind of situation is rare and won't happen with the main high street lenders.

Traditionally, parents have often guaranteed loans for children. Theoretically, role reversal could operate with, say, someone aged 40 guaranteeing a mortgage taken out by a 75-year-old parent. Most lenders have pulled out of the guarantor market, however (probably because it's a much-needed one and they would be swamped) and those remaining in it will insist the guarantor is a blood relative. The age of the oldest applicant will also come into play, and the loan term itself would be very short.

Some mortgage lenders will require a bigger deposit for a new-build flat or house (being uneasy about over-inflated values on new-build properties). It's very hard to get a normal mortgage on a flat above commercial premises, and pretty much impossible to get one on a flat which is not leasehold. (A house can be leasehold or freehold.) Solicitors may charge more for the conveyancing on a leasehold property.

The construction of the property itself is important to note as some lenders won't lend on timber-framed structures, for example, or on a lot of the houses built soon after the Second World War, which were concrete structures. Incidentally, there should be no sex discrimination in granting mortgages, provided the sums make sense.

Despite all the media stories of property scandals, it is still possible to get a mortgage for a property abroad. There are a number of brokers that deal with overseas mortgages. The high street banks may have arms for this, but their criteria tend to

be a bit tight. Overseas mortgages will normally require larger deposits, say 30% to 40%.

Retirement villages? The developers will usually have a deal with a specific lender. Lenders don't particularly like them, mainly because of the way that the properties themselves can, in certain instances, sometimes revert back to the developer. A lender wants 100% charge and they have to be sure that if a default occurs they could take the property and sell it easily and quickly to get their money back.

If you have a property with a mortgage, it will be OK to rent it out while you go and live somewhere else provided you tell your lender. Some lenders will issue a consent-to-let form, while others will just say 'no problem'. However, it has been occasionally known for some lenders to take the view that this is a reason to put your rate up, or just charge a fee to issue a letter saying OK to the arrangement. The main thing is to ensure that your insurance company is aware that the property is let; you can get a specific 'landlords' insurance' through most insurance companies.

Equity release schemes – perhaps to pay for care – have had a very poor press and are a 'grey' area. The general feeling is that they are expensive in both fees and rates because hardly any mainstream lenders offer them and so competition is weak. An equity release scheme may be based on a minimum age of, say, 60 and for every five years above that you can release a higher percentage of your equity; the interest is rolled up and paid either on death or when the property is sold. They are, unfortunately, pretty much the only option open to releasing funds from your home to pay for care, so even if they're not worthwhile there may not be another choice. If someone is moving out of their home to go into care, depending on their age etc., it may be possible for them to re-mortgage the house on a buy-to-let mortgage, releasing the required equity that way and renting it out, which means they then get the money and the loan is being paid off.

As if all that wasn't confusing enough, there are various types of mortgage.

A fixed rate mortgage gives you the ability to budget, and peace of mind. Whatever happens to the base rate, and rates in general, yours won't change – your monthly payment will stay the same – but if rates drop, yours won't.

A tracker mortgage is directly linked to the Bank of England base rate and will be set at a percentage level above base, so if base rate goes up then your rate increases too. At the moment these mortgages are popular, but they don't offer the ability to budget and they do leave you open to market forces. Someone on a tight budget may not have the room to soak up any upward movements in the base rate itself.

Every lender has a standard variable rate mortgage option and these are set by themselves. They tend to be their highest rates and the ones which one reverts to after the end of any deal (such as at the end of a two-year fixed rate deal). In 99% of cases they will not have 'tie ins', which means that the individual has a lot more freedom to overpay and can leave that lender without incurring an early repayment charge.

What's best for an oldie? It really depends on your budget, personal circumstances, short-term future regarding moving house/job/pension and so on, as well as your attitude to risk.

Points to bear in mind

- Make mortgage overpayments if you can, in order to reduce the debt; many deals allow you to overpay by up to 10%. If interest rates are on the floor, it doesn't make sense to store money away earning peanuts – it would be better to use it to bring forward the glorious day when you become mortgage-free.

- It's a tough market out there. Any stains on your financial record, such as difficulty with a credit card, could adversely affect your chances of getting a mortgage.

- Use a broker. They can advise you on everyone's products and this may give you a better chance of getting the most suitable mortgage for your circumstances; a bank will only offer you their products. If you do go directly to a bank, perhaps get a quote and then let a broker trawl the whole market for you.

- Be cautious of special mortgage deals where the interest rate skyrockets when the deal ends. A good broker will contact you a couple of months before this happens to ensure that you don't go on to a high rate and will instead re-mortgage you to another lender with a competitive rate.

- Keep lenders in the picture if your circumstances change.

- Keep all paperwork.

- Take into account any set-up fees that the lender will add to the loan at the outset, because a cheap rate with a high fee may not actually be the most cost effective over the scheme's term (two years, for example), especially if the loan is relatively small.

- Yes, you really can lose your home if you don't keep up the payments.

Income tax

- Keep records. You are supposed to keep them for seven years, but if you made a property transaction earlier than that then it may be sensible to keep the key documents for longer.

- Keep invoices, bank statements, paying-in slips to show where any income has come from, receipts for purchases and other expenses, dividend voucher counterfoils, records of any share dealings and so on. Also keep documents confirming contributions to pension schemes plus a record of any charity giving, whether by deed of covenant or Gift Aid.

- Filling in a tax form online is quite straightforward as, some would say unfortunately, it is to pay online. Go to www.hmrc.gov.uk

- File your return on time. Being one day late attracts a penalty, even if there is no tax to pay or you have already paid all the tax you owe. There will be further penalties if you are then late in paying any tax due.

- In any tax year you can give away ('gift') up to £250 to as many individuals as you like. Single gifts can be given to a total of £3,000 over a tax year. If you don't give the full £3,000 in one tax year you can carry any balance over to the next one (but only for one year).

- It is also possible to make regular 'gifts from income'. If you can prove that by giving more than the regulated £3,000 per year you are not reducing your own standard of living, and that you can afford it, then HMRC is content to see that you are giving more away. By definition, this could reduce the amount of estate duty (inheritance tax) in the long run.

Inheritance tax (IHT)

Talk about it! You need total trust before giving money away to use the seven-year rule (i.e. if you live for longer than seven years after making a gift, there is no tax liability on that gift). At least the thought of a likely legacy may mean relatives keep in touch.

- Currently IHT is 40% on estates of more than £325,000. If you bequeath all your assets to your wife/husband, no IHT has to be paid. You need a savvy solicitor on board so that twice the IHT-free allowance can be bequeathed to family members on the second death before HMRC get their hands on any of the residue.

- On death, IHT is payable by the estate. Gifts made within seven years are added back, but a sliding scale which kicks in after three years reduces their value. All assets are valued and executors have to sign a declaration that everything has been included, to the best of their knowledge.

- Under a scheme known as Legacy 10, those making a charitable donation of 10% or more of their estate will have the IHT on the rest of their estate reduced from 40% to 36% – 'ten for ten', i.e. a 10% reduction of IHT in return for a 10% donation. But take care – do your sums carefully first or you could leave children/grandchildren worse off.

Keep records. You are supposed to keep them for seven years, but if you made a property transaction earlier than that then it may be sensible to keep documents for longer.

Ethical or green investing? It's your call. Or investing in 'new' countries? Well, if you get in early the rewards can be great – but so can the losses.

Capital gains tax (CGT)

Currently you can make profits of £10,600 in each tax year before CGT is paid.

Above this figure, tax is at 18% (or 28% if you pay higher-rate tax).

If you are planning on selling assets like shares it makes sense to spread disposals over the years in order to avoid CGT.

VAT

Don't take this lightly – the VAT people can make Rotweillers look effeminate.

Investing

- Whatever you invest in, be clear on your aims and objectives. Decide whether to adopt a fail-safe investment strategy (or at least as safe as is possible) or a more adventurous one. If the latter, keep your crystal ball highly polished.

- Invest in areas you understand, perhaps through your job or a hobby. Or maybe invest in products aimed at the elderly – clearly a growth market!

- Try to probe the risks of anything you are considering investing in, whether shares, art, fine wine, or whatever. If the promised returns sound too good to be true, it's probably because they are.

- Are you knowledgeable about finance or will you need help? If the latter, be clear on what fees and commissions are being charged by advisers as there can be rip-offs. The Financial Services Authority (FSA) states that every financial adviser must give prospective clients a 'key facts' document, spelling out charges and commissions. Make sure you get one in writing.

- Guard against being charged for services you didn't receive. If you bought funds online or by phone, for instance, yet were charged for financial advice you didn't actually receive.

- Keep records and monitor any investments you make. One advantage of retirement is that it may give you time to do this.

Shares

- Remember that what goes up…

- Decide whether to spread your investments with a balanced portfolio or go for broke with just one.

- Ethical or green investing? It's your call. Or investing in 'new' countries? Well, if you get in early the rewards can be great – but so can the losses.

- Consider carefully any shareholder perks such as discounts.

- Beware of boiler room scams – unsolicited calls, emails or letters from overseas-based brokers offering to sell you something that will prove to be worthless or very high risk. These always sound very plausible – and it is not just investment novices who are caught by such people. Stating that you are recording a phone sales pitch may help bring it to an abrupt end.

- Beware, too, of bogus selling via websites. It is too easy to make such sites look professional and honest. (Sorry about all the references to websites, by the way, but that's where lie the delights … and dangers.) Check that a company is properly authorised by the Financial Services Authority (FSA) by going to www.fsa.gov.uk/register and make sure you get the correct name of the person and the organisation.

- Look too at the FSA website www.moneymadeclear.fsa.gov.uk where you can get plenty of advice on what shares to buy and when. Just as important, though, is knowing when to *sell*:

  - Is the share still performing as you had hoped?
  - Has your aim in buying the share been achieved, e.g. before a takeover?
  - Don't fall in love with a share. Beware of throwing good money after bad; it may be better to cut your losses.

National Savings are a guaranteed secure investment, with no tax on interest, although the government can change the terms of interest with immediate effect.

Individual savings accounts (ISAs)

These accounts help you escape the clutches of the taxman because they allow you to save and earn interest without paying any tax, as well as to invest in stocks and shares without being taxed on any returns you make. There is a wide range of ISA products available, basically within two main types – cash ISAs, which are like a savings account and for which you could set up a standing order to pay in every month up to the annual limit and stocks and shares ISAs through which you can invest in funds or the stock market with the possibility of higher returns. You could set up a standing order to pay into either type of ISA every month up to the annual limit. You can only contribute to one of each per person, per tax year. Some companies will also take your lump sum and phase this into investment over a period of time as opportunities occur e.g. into 'medium risk' investments or whatever you stipulate.

For the 2012–13 tax year you can invest up to a maximum of £11,280 (double that for a husband and wife) and pay no CGT or further income tax on any income.

What's best for you will depend on your personal circumstances, and these should be taken into account by ISA managers, which include banks, building societies, financial advisers, etc. who must be authorised by the Financial Services Authority (FSA). That may be no guarantee of performance, but it does provide access to a complaints procedure if things go wrong.

Other investment possibilities

- The Enterprise Investment Scheme was designed by the government to help smaller companies obtain finance by providing investors with incentives to invest in smaller unquoted companies; they are free of CGT if held for three years and outside IHT if held for two. Professional advice is strongly recommended in this area.

- Trusts such as Discounted Gift Trusts (where there are many possible advantages, provided the correct procedures are followed) also need professional advice, or if you are investing in Venture Capital Trusts. The VCT scheme is intended to encourage individuals to invest indirectly in a range of small, higher-risk trading companies (whose shares and securities are not listed on a recognised stock exchange). By investing through VCTs you can spread the investment over a number of companies.

- Premium Bonds are something the novice investor may prefer (although there are tax benefits with all the above). Premium Bonds pay no interest, but the money is safe and, of course, you have the excitement of opening an envelope occasionally … it may only be a small win, but at least it's free of tax. Keep a record of any winnings and calculate how they compare if you'd kept your money in a deposit account instead.

- National Savings are also a guaranteed secure investment, with no tax on interest, although the government can change the terms of interest with immediate effect.

Alternative investments

Keep in mind that with many alternative investments you may not be able to convert assets into cash quickly if you hit an emergency. Although property can provide revenue in the form of rent, you may only make money from other alternatives through capital appreciation when you sell.

Property

- There are ups and downs in property prices, just as there are with shares, but property is an attractive investment area for many people because most feel they know at least something about it and, unlike purely financial investments, you can actually 'see' what you own.

- You will get tax relief on the repair and running costs of a buy-to-let property as well as on loan interest payments, plus a wear and tear allowance of 10% of the rents you receive. There may be CGT to pay when you sell a buy-to-let property, however.

- Follow the rules about employing qualified trade people for gas and electrical work. It's not a DIY area.

- Get hold of the free *Landlord and Buy-to-Let* magazine which has useful news and advice.

- Research the area where you are thinking of buying to let. Flats in towns may be best, houses in the countryside.

- Using a management company can mean a lot less hassle. Yes, of course you can manage a property yourself, but it helps to have someone up to speed with the rules and regulations and to find and interface with tenants. A managing agent will also handle deposits, an area that causes many rental problems. Check if the management company is in an organisation like ARLA (the Association of Residential Letting Agents) so that you may make progress if you have a complaint.

- Local agents will advise if it is better to let furnished or unfurnished. This doesn't seem to make much difference to occupancy levels in many areas.

- Advise the agent if you do not want smokers or pets in the property.

- Let your insurance company know you are renting out the property.

- References should always be taken up for prospective tenants, either by you or your agent.

- Rent out on a 'shorthold tenancy' basis so that you have a guaranteed right to get the place back after a stipulated time, provided the proper procedures are followed. It is important to play it by the book because, with a shortage of houses to let, local authorities may not be able to help your tenants if you are trying to move them out.

- You will have to provide an EPC (Energy Performance Certificate) for a property to be let. These certificates last for ten years.

- In many areas you will need a licence from the local authority if you are letting an HMO (house in multiple occupation). Rules on this tend to be getting stricter.

- Don't screw the very last penny out of tenants. A gentler approach may help your place be treated better. Sadly, not all places are treated well. It is not unknown for tenants to turn places into cannabis farms or even take batteries out of smoke alarms to power other things (so perhaps it would be wise to fit tamper-proof ones).

- Spell out any ground rules before a let, such as no Blu-Tack on the walls.

- You or your agent should do inventories with clear photographs at the start and end of tenancies to avoid arguments. Note any pre-damage on the photographs (which should be good quality prints) and date them. Include something that gives scale to a photograph; this helps if arguing later over how large a wine stain is on a carpet.

- Take care that a relative – perhaps a grandchild – doesn't become bogged down in landlord duties if living with others in any student accommodation you own.

- Rent in arrears? Act firmly if debt keeps running up. Eviction may be the only answer in the end, but don't take the law into your own hands. You can't force your way back in and you will have to go to court. It can take several weeks to get an eviction order and the law doesn't appear to be applied consistently across the country.

Local agents will advise if it is better to let furnished or unfurnished. This doesn't seem to make much difference to occupancy levels in many areas.

Tax relief will only apply if a property is available for letting for 210 days a year and is actually let for at least 105 of those days.

• Squatting is not illegal at the time of writing, although there are moves to make it so. It costs money to evict squatters and repair likely damage, but you can't go round with a bunch of large, menacing gentlemen and turf people out, and the police may be reluctant to get involved, especially if it means putting families on to the street. Negotiation may be the best starting point.

Holiday lets

These can be very profitable in popular areas, although there may be more hassle than with longer-term tenants, as well as more wear and tear. Tax relief will only apply if a property is available for letting for 210 days a year and is actually let for at least 105 of those days. (This should be readily achievable in popular areas.) Moreover, no single let must be for longer than a month. Local councils may have varying rules, too.

Whether you invest in property for long-term or holiday letting, and if you are tempted to buy at auction:

Always inspect before bidding and check the planning situation, if applicable.

Decide on your maximum bid and then stick to it. When the hammer falls, you've bought it, whatever problems suddenly appear. You will have to pay a 10% deposit, with the balance in 28 days – and you are responsible for insurance in that time.

Other alternatives

• If you feel like investing in land that is 'sure' to get planning permission and leap in value, like a field marked out in building plots, lie down until the feeling goes away.

• Collectable items can make money, but do study books on antiques etc. and do your homework, whether on pottery, furniture, stamps, medals, coins or whatever. Learn, for instance, that the box housing a collector's model may be as important as the item itself. Knowledge is power and retirement may give you time to acquire it.

Left: The box can be as important as the collectable item.

- It will be interesting to see what effect the move to e-books will have on the market for books, but specialised ones may show useful appreciation.

- Don't get over-optimistic or excited about values. The £1 boot sale purchase selling at auction for £100,000 is actually quite rare.

- Wine may be regarded as a wasting asset by the tax authorities, if it is believed to have a life of less than 50 years – in which case it is free of capital gains tax.

  - Do a blind taste of any wine you are planning to invest in, comparing it with lower-priced wines. Blind tests often show that many people can't tell the difference. (And isn't it a joy when some of them are revealed to be so-called 'experts'?)
  - There may be a risk of fake wines, too, because it may not be what it says on the label. Not everyone is prepared to admit to being duped, so word may not spread.
    If you decide to go ahead with a wine investment company, compare fees for setting up your investment portfolio and storing it in a fully insured, bonded warehouse – and be clear on annual management fees.
  - With climate change you may be tempted to produce your own wine, but it will take time – several years – to establish a vineyard.
  - At least with wine you can always drink your investment – as you can if you invest instead in a micro-brewery.

- Unless you have specialised knowledge of a particular artist, collect art that you really like so that you get enjoyment from it, even if there is not quite the hoped-for capital appreciation.

- Some people feel that gold and diamonds hold their value when times are tough, but you will need to take expert advice about either.

- With autographed items and other memorabilia, beware of fakes. The sheer number of these is why some people prefer items dedicated to people. A signature in a book or on a photograph – 'To Gladys with thanks for the apple pie' – may seem trite, but it is likely to be genuine. As with some antiques, timing may be important if selling something linked to a famous name. It may actually fall in value if their fame fades over time.

- Being a 'Theatre Angel' or helping finance a film may sound a glamorous investment, and various schemes may be available from time to time to appeal to investors, but this is not an area for the novice. Don't get swept away by the thought of meeting the stars.

Insurance

Last but most emphatically not least in this money section – insurance. I have only put it at the end because the previous things discussed may affect what insurance you need. Your insurance needs may change on retirement in any case – if, say, you lose the cushion of a company car or a health plan but also no longer have financial responsibility for your children.

It is vital to understand that many financial products designed for the older market are based upon a short time period and are not insurance in the conventional sense.

Conventional insurance works on the assumption that lots of people contribute to a pot of money, and the unlucky few who are hit by misfortune receive a significant payout. Products designed for older clients are based on the assumption that the misfortune will happen to a lot of clients and there is not a big enough pool of contributors, so your payout is likely to be near the sum of your premiums, less the provider's expenses.

A second and equally important point is that non-disclosures can be an insurance company's main get-out – and rightly so. If you get cheaper insurance by 'missing out' a piece of information that influences your premium that constitutes attempted fraud, and the insurance company is right to walk away.

Some people feel that gold and diamonds hold their value when times are tough, but you will need to take expert advice about either.

Health insurance

Private health care schemes can be expensive. An underlying problem is that the later you join, the higher the initial premiums. Just to add to the pain, premiums will certainly increase year on year at a rate significantly faster than inflation.

Whether to take out cover or not may depend on your confidence in the local NHS. Ask friends for their experience if they have used the NHS in your catchment area. Health is one of many areas where personal recommendation can be a good guide. I know of two neighbours who had the same operation in the same ward in the same hospital with the same surgeon. One was NHS, the other private. They received identical service. The only difference was that the private patient was treated slightly sooner, but only because she was in pain.

Instead of taking out cover you may decide to put the same amount of money away each month into your own 'health fund', provided you know you have the discipline to maintain its status.

If you do take out health insurance, premiums may be lower if you agree to a higher excess, i.e. how much you pay for each claim, although once in retirement it may have to be a massive excess to reduce the premium noticeably. Some schemes may offer no-claims bonuses, although premiums could then shoot up if you do make a claim.

If you sign up for a private scheme:

● Will you face having to make financial top-ups?
● Will pre-existing medical conditions be covered? They may not be covered for some time, if ever, for conditions that you have previously consulted a doctor about.
● Will you be able to choose the hospital and doctor?

With health cash plans you pay an insurance company a monthly premium, then when you pay for certain treatment you can reclaim a percentage of the costs from the company. Most such plans only cover part of the cost of your treatment and there will be an annual limit. You yourself need to make the claim, getting a claim form stamped by the person who treated you. Keep receipts, of course. Such schemes only help with the cost; you have to find the medical service providers or therapists for yourself.

Will pre-existing medical conditions be covered? They may not be covered for some time, if ever, for conditions that you have previously consulted a doctor about.

Life insurance

These may be considered as glorified savings plans with high administrative costs, but you may decide on one either as a cash gift for loved ones or to help with your funeral costs. If you are in such a scheme for, say, a couple of years, it will pay out a fixed sum on your death. If you die before the two years are up, the premiums will be returned.

Acceptance is usually guaranteed without a medical or answering questions about your health, perhaps because the provider's calculations assume all the clients will die during the life of the policy.

Any fixed sum for which you are insured will reduce in value because of inflation, and if you live a long time you may have paid more in premiums than will be paid out. But whether you would have tucked the same amount away each month is another matter.

Third party liability

In these litigious times everyone should have third party liability to cover any incidents connected with their residence. It is worth checking that your home insurance has this included. The better policies include your liability off-site and some even include the actions of your dog or when you are out cycling.

Accident insurance

These are limited products to cover injury due to an accident. However, they need checking as the cheaper versions may exclude accidents as a result of illness. So if you fall over and break a hip because you tripped then you are covered, but if you faint and fall over you are not.

Travel insurance

The most important part of a travel policy is the bit most people ignore – the cover for medical treatment and repatriation; 10% of travellers don't bother with cover, and of course there is nothing to stop you doing the same. But it is a brave step, or rather a foolish one, especially if travelling to countries with high medical costs. Where you are visiting will affect the premium you pay. To treat a stroke and then return a patient to the UK from the USA will cost the price of a small house.

Most insurers have a cap on the age of those they will insure, while travel insurance packaged with bank accounts or credit cards may also have age limits. As the media tend to focus on poor experiences in this area, here is a good one: a broker took less than a day to find travel insurance for me, at the age of 78, for a long Oz trip. I got stuck there for a week because of volcanic ash. The company paid out quickly without a murmur.

It may seem crazy that travel insurance premiums double overnight when, say, you move from 65 to 66, but in fact at 65 lots of men retire and go for one long adventure holiday and do things they should not really attempt.

It is important to declare any medical condition – this may involve a phone discussion with a nurse. If any non-disclosure is discovered later, the company won't pay.

Buildings and contents insurance

- If you have two separate policies, a building and a contents cover, investigate having one joint product as this is often cheaper.

- If you have a second home – maybe one you plan to move to later in retirement, which is often unoccupied – insurers may insist that you visit it at least once a month.

- Properties rented out also need specialist policies.

- While it may cost more, you should seriously consider having accident cover for both building and contents.

Pet insurance

This is one form of insurance which may be essential for older pet owners with limited means. The cost is relatively low but the peace of mind is invaluable, knowing it may avoid having to choose between a pet's life and dwindling savings.

Motor insurance

The biggest part of motor insurance is to pay for compensation to others injured by your car. It is not the small injuries; if a young victim is rendered totally paralysed the compensation may run into millions.

As drivers get older the risk of an accident will at first decline and premiums will reduce, but then you will reach a point when the risk starts to increase, and with it the premium. Sadly, this is true for all of us. At the end of each year your existing insurer is required to offer you terms, but they can increase the premium if they consider that you are an increased risk. At this point you may be trapped, as other insurers may also consider you have moved into the increased risk zone and will not wish to offer you terms.

For standard road cars the internet is your best friend. Spend some time collecting quotes from two or three comparison sites plus a couple of the direct websites. If you do not have internet skills, co-opt a younger member of the family.

If your vehicle is specialised or you can't find car cover then turn to an insurance broker who could contact specialist insurance companies.

Any quote may depend on where you live – there are black spots – as well as your occupation, if you are still working. If you do a low annual mileage, say so.

Are you an oldie boy or girl racer? Modifying your car will increase the premium.

Garaging it will lower the cost because there will be less chance of damage and theft, although with the advent of decent locks, alarms and immobilisers this is becoming less true.

If you have a second home – maybe one you plan to move to later in retirement, which is often unoccupied – insurers may insist that you visit it at least once a month.

Check the insurance group of a new car before buying. Include your partner on the policy. You may benefit from the 'family factor' because you may be considered to drive more sensibly if a loved one is with you. Remember that putting yourself down as a driver, when in fact a child or grandchild is doing the driving, in order to reduce premiums, is fraud and could invalidate the terms of a policy. And get you accustomed to prison food.

Identity theft cover

Beware being over-sold this. It is easy to portray it as a 'shock horror' crime but the number of people actually making claims is low. Take sensible precautions and save your money instead. You may be covered by banks and so forth for many problems.

Product cover

When shopping, whether for a mobile phone or a fridge freezer, do not feel that you *have* to buy insurance, or add-on warranties. Salesmen's commission can be the driver and, not surprisingly, there have been many complaints.

Finally, whatever the insurance

- Beware of insurers renewing policies automatically because of what is written in the small print. You may lose an opportunity to move to a better deal – and it is always worth querying any sudden increase in your premium. (And isn't it infuriating when companies offer better deals to new customers than they do to reliable old ones?)

- The large print giveth … the small print taketh away. I found one of my policies even had a 'Reincarnation Clause' – if I die and come back I have to bring the money with me…

- To stress an earlier point, whatever the insurance, don't lie. If you get caught out, insurance thenceforth will be a problem. And that applies to all insurance – fiddle your holiday insurance and your car insurance will rocket.

YOU AND YOUR HOME

Remaining in your home

Retirement may be the time to tackle all those jobs around the home that have been building up over the years, or to do a major remodelling of your property. Doing such work may be a good way of helping to adjust to retirement. If you are likely to sell your home and move later then increasing floor space, such as converting a loft into living space or adding a conservatory, will add value. But before you start digging, keep in mind that you probably won't recoup the cost of a swimming pool, although having one may help you to keep fit.

If it is your first try at remodelling or planning something new:

● Plan for what your needs might be in the future, e.g. for wheelchair access.

● Decide exactly what you want before starting work. Changing your mind half way through is not an economical way of building.

● Plan for adequate lighting, not least to avoid falls as you get older.

● Consider safety. A DIY project may seem as easy as falling off a ladder. And that's the problem – every year many people, both young and old, injure themselves doing just that.

● Use the project as a reason to de-clutter. Apparently, compulsive hoarding is now a recognised disorder.

● Assume costs will always be higher than expected so build a healthy contingency sum into your calculations.

● If you are using a builder, agree a stage payment plan in advance and then pay on time; building a sound relationship may enhance your chances of getting a problem fixed more easily later.

● Keep a diary of progress and retain invoices in case of any disputes.

'The property slump has really hit hard around here.'

Ken Pyne

Moving on retirement

Your lifestyle leading up to retirement may affect whether you decide to move or not. Someone in a routine job and with few interests may find retirement to a seaside bungalow more appealing than someone with a busy lifestyle they hope to maintain. If you are planning to move on retirement, perhaps because you are rattling around in a property that is too big, then:

● Draw up a shopping list of the things you value most – nightlife, tranquillity, the countryside, easy access to motorways or whatever.

● If you have the funds, perhaps consider a second home in an area to 'test' it before you move there permanently. But check local regulations carefully as some cash-struck councils threaten attacks on second homes.

● Visiting the local pub and church may help give you a feel for a new place.

● Moving to the country may not be all you expected. Transport costs can be higher, while if the place is within an hour or so of a major city beware of 'weekday blight' when the place becomes a ghost village during the week because the weekenders have gone back to the city.

● If you have a survey done of a property before buying, establish with the surveyor exactly what level of survey you want and draw attention to any particular points you want checking.

● If research into the area reveals a risk of flooding, run (or swim) a mile.

● If you're still uncertain whether a place is right for you, spending a few months in a rental property can be an excellent way of establishing whether you want to live there permanently.

Draw up a shopping list of the things you value most – nightlife, tranquillity, the countryside, easy access to motorways or whatever.

Retirement developments

This sort of accommodation can provide home ownership, with your own front door but without the hassle of repairs or garden maintenance. A few points to keep in mind:

● How many properties in the development are still for sale? There may be a dismal atmosphere if many are unsold.

● Is parking adequate for both residents and visitors?

● Service charges? Read the small print. It has been known for contractors employed to work on a development to be linked to the managing agents so that residents do not get the best value.

● There can also be greedy freeholders and management agents eager to add whatever charges they can. The key is to support any residents' association, take no nonsense and if necessary consult the Rights to Manage Federation about removing the managing agent.

● Would you face extra charges if you sublet? Such charges can sometimes be as a percentage of the capital value and might make a deal unviable.

● What exit fees might you face if you leave a development?

Mobile homes

One of these could be an alternative to a more conventional residence, either as a permanent home or if you want to test an area. If you are having something built then living on the site in a mobile home may work, especially if you can have it connected to water, electricity and drainage.

If you are in a 'posh' area you may hear sniffs at the arrival of a caravan. I found a cure when I experienced this while having a house built – a friend lent me a Rolls-Royce for a few days, which I parked ostentatiously alongside the caravan. End of sniffs.

If you buy a mobile home on a park, check the position regarding holiday rentals if, say, you want to travel for a while and earn some revenue in your absence. And also check the exit situation if you want to leave as there may be various buy-back clauses. Disputes are not uncommon.

Co-operative schemes

You may decide to live with relatives when you've retired, or you may consider a co-operative housing scheme. It can be argued that a dozen or so people sharing a large house would save money and make friends. But – and it is a large but – there can be problems so:

● Consult existing groups to discover the ups and the downsides.

● Have crystal-clear rules, which must be written down. The more people in a house, the more chances of disputes, so this point is absolutely essential.

● Have regular residents' meeting and flag up issues before they become major concerns.

● Who controls the remote control if there is a residents' lounge?

Moving abroad

This is the dream of many retirees, with the prospect of endless golf, an equable climate and lower heating costs, but it's not without pitfalls. Don't just drool over holiday photographs, take a less rosy view and consider the following:

● Although the major change involved may stimulate the brain, it will mean leaving the places and people you know.

● Will cheap flights always be available to the nearest airport?

· ·

Would you face extra charges if you sublet? Such charges can sometimes be as a percentage of the capital value and might make a deal unviable.

As in the UK, property prices can go down as well as up; 50% falls are not uncommon, with some properties proving difficult or impossible to sell.

- What care will be on hand if your health deteriorates? Will you qualify for local care and will there be access to English-speaking medical people?

- Be clear what effect, if any, a move abroad would have on your pension. In some countries you may not receive annual inflation increases on a UK pension, which could cause havoc over time.

- How might exchange rate changes affect you?

- If your chosen country hits problems (and what country doesn't nowadays?) it may impose tax rules that you have not anticipated, such as a new property tax or even one on the number of sun umbrellas you are allowed.

- As in the UK, property prices can go down as well as up; 50% falls are not uncommon, with some properties proving difficult or impossible to sell.

- Visit your chosen place in the off-season when tourist facilities are closed. That may be the time most burglaries happen (and can be one of the main reasons why people sell their holiday homes). Buying in a community which is 'live' all year round will be preferable.

- If you settle in a place with a lot of other Brits you may find yourself settling into a routine of too much alcohol while reminiscing about real ale and fish and chips. Conversely, if you are the only Brit then you may make friends because you are something of a novelty. Learning the language will undoubtedly help the process.

Right: Extreme measures may be needed if you buy property in an area prone to flooding.

Renting out what you own could be a nice earner while you roam in retirement. Tax is payable on rents, of course, but your expenses can be offset.

- What will your exit strategy be if the move abroad goes wrong? If you've burnt all your boats (and talking of boats, have you considered a canal barge for retirement?), it may be quite difficult – not least in getting back on to the UK property ladder.

But if, despite all these concerns, you decide to go ahead and buy abroad then be sure to get translations of any legal documents; always have someone with you at meetings to interpret for you; and don't sign anything unless you have consulted a lawyer with experience in that country (they should be registered with the equivalent of the Law Society in the UK).

Thinking of a timeshare? Think again. There are too many people already trapped in expensive deals for life. Some contracts may even pass on to your next-of-kin, while some unlucky timesharers have been conned a second time by people offering to offload their 'shares' for them. Perhaps it's not surprising that in some places the resale market simply isn't there.

If you move abroad and want to take your pet you will find that if, say, your dog is microchipped against rabies and given a blood test to ensure protection is adequate, then you can get a passport for the animal. Your vet will be able to advise on this and also on whether there is anything to be wary of for the pet in the country you have chosen.

Renting

Renting for a while may be useful, in order to test an area before a permanent move, although you may be gambling on property prices. If they fall then they are not your problem, but if they leap up you may, like people returning from retirement abroad, struggle to get back on to the property ladder.

Renting out what you own could be a nice earner while you roam in retirement. Tax is payable on rents, of course, but your expenses can be offset.

If you rent out, do note the points on investing in property detailed in the previous chapter on money matters.

Selling what you have

You can sell a property yourself, but using an estate agent may make the process smoother and less stressful and will put the property in front of a wider audience. Finding an estate agent? Note sold signs in the area and use word of mouth. Estate agents have been overtaken by bankers and politicians in the list of Those We Love To Hate, but there are still complaints to the Property Ombudsman so it is worth selecting one with care. The biggest problem seems to be poor communication, so it obviously helps if the estate agent is someone you get on with.

'You're going for a start!'

Keep in mind the following:

- Getting planning permission, perhaps on a disused area of the garden, may increase the property's value. If there is 'hope' of planning being given some time in the future, then insert a clause in the sales documents that you will receive X% of any increase in value should planning be obtained within a given number of years.

- If you sign a sole selling rights agreement with an estate agent, but then do a deal yourself via personal contacts or the internet, you will almost certainly still have to pay the agent's fees.

- Visit one or two properties similar to yours to study the competition. People used to constant house price rises may find it difficult to accept that the figure they are expecting is hopelessly optimistic. Having some awareness of local prices may stop you falling for an estate agent who deliberately overvalues your property simply to get the job.

- Accentuate the positives when selling, but don't lie. Being open about even trivial faults may stop a sale falling through at the last minute, with one of the faults being used as an excuse.

- A Seller's Property Information form will comprise part of the conveyancing process. If you don't mention something that a vendor had a right to know – such as a problem with neighbours – then you could be sued later.

- Last-minute gazumpers? Keep your property on the market until contracts have actually been exchanged.

MODERN TECHNOLOGY

More than three-quarters of over 65s now own a computer and are online, but that still leaves quite a lot of people to convert – hence this chapter. Not being online is becoming a bit like saying you haven't got running water. Those who are not connected will be increasingly disadvantaged as more products and services only become available in this way.

Don't be afraid of the technology, or the jargon that goes with it. Most of it is quite straightforward (like WYSIWIG which stands for What You See Is What You Get). You can't physically hurt yourself with the technology – unless, of course, you pull a muscle hurling a computer at the wall in frustration, as you may well be tempted to do at times. And it is never too late to start; I know of one lady who sent her first email when she was 98.

Computers

If you are a novice, look for computer advice couched in plain English and try to get a clued-up friend or relative to help. Perhaps cut your teeth on a computer in a local library or attend a computer course geared to the 'over 50s' or 'beginners'.

A desktop machine may be a better choice than a laptop (unless you are always on the move) because the keyboards are easier to use and the screens are generally bigger. A pair of speakers is a useful addition; you will pay extra for the quality of your sound.

You don't have to have the latest technology; bargains can be had from companies that specialise in getting rid of old stock which has just been superseded. Mind you, while at first you may gaze in awe at a computer, within a week you may be shouting at it to go faster.

Shop around before you buy a computer and, most importantly, think about after-sales service. I'm glad I bought mine from a local supplier who calls and fixes the confounded thing if, or rather when, I manage to freeze it.

All computers will have an operating system installed. This tells the computer how to work and will almost invariably be a software called Windows. Applications software are applications you can add to your computer, either via disk or by downloading from the internet. They can help with anything you can imagine, whether keeping your accounts, playing games like Solitaire, or writing a book.

There is a lot of adaptive equipment and software available to help those with disabilities such as limited mobility in the hands, while with voice recognition software you can dictate your words instead of typing them.

> Don't just look at the first page which pops up when you search a subject, because you may miss possible gems on later pages.

Connecting to the internet

You will need to register with an internet service provider (ISP). Regarding speed, with broadband connections now available everywhere, this will depend on the level of service you buy from your ISP and generally not on the speed of your computer. Speed also depends on how far you are from the telephone exchange. If you plan to become an online gamer, or want to watch TV over the internet, you will require a faster speed, but for many people the basic broadband services will be more than adequate.

Access to all the information is by using search engines such as Google, Bing, Ask Jeeves, Yahoo (the list is long). Don't just look at the first page which pops up when you search a subject, because you may miss possible gems on later pages.

Websites

If you are involved with, say, a social club or a lobbying campaign, then creating a website may be worthwhile. It's not really complicated and there is plenty of online help available. The objective should be to convey information or enthuse people, not to show how clever you are with the technology. I'm not the only one turned off by sites with tap-dancing dogs or waltzing elephants flitting across the screen. And remember that garbage is still garbage even if you put 'dot.com' after it.

Email

As the name suggests, emails are simply messages sent via electronic means rather than through the post. You can register with a free email service such as Yahoo, Hotmail or Google. There are a lot out there.

The computer undoubtedly makes communication quicker, but it does not help you differentiate between what is passingly important and what is really urgent. Emails can make everything feel 'hurry, hurry', so the most important piece of advice is to pause before pressing 'send'. It is all too easy to send an email too soon or to the wrong people. Research has suggested that simply being online can lower your inhibitions to a level equal to having had a couple of drinks. So take care!

Social networking sites

Social networking is the grouping of individuals into specific groups, like small rural communities or a neighbourhood. Caution is needed with sites such as Facebook, where you can add 'friends'. You may find yourself adding someone you wouldn't normally speak to, so you end up pretending to be 'friends' with people who, if they knocked on your door, would make you hide under the kitchen table.

Social networking can be useful, however, not least on a local level for sharing information about events. You might have a site, say, for a Scrabble or bowls club that can be viewed by anyone, although only members of the club can actually 'post' items on to the page. In this way members can share views, experiences and information about events while the more general access may help attract new members.

Forums

These may be formed for members of a particular organisation or by angry users of a poor product. They are regarded by some not as 'chat' rooms but as 'prat' rooms, because the drivel put on to a few of them may make you long for a Dafter Protection Act; they can be likened to listening to bores in the corner of a pub bar. Making people use their real names may reduce vitriol on forums.

YouTube

This is a video-sharing website, and includes movie and TV clips, and music videos, as well as amateur content. YouTube is an excellent source for finding your favourite old TV programmes, songs or historical newsreels. It all seems to be there.

*'Hang on while I tweet that I'm telling
you to hang on while I tweet.'*

Blogs

Blogs are 'editorial' pieces where writers give their own views on a particular subject. They are usually the work of a single individual, occasionally of a small group, and are often themed on a single subject.

Twitter was created as a forum for short bursts of inconsequential information using (mercifully) a maximum of 140 characters, hence 'twitter' like the chirping of birds. It is a free service under which you can send messages – 'tweets' – and it can give you a link to a favourite celebrity, although if you really, really want to know what someone famous had for breakfast … shouldn't you get out more? Maybe the celebrities should get out more, too, because over-communication can destroy mystique. By the way, celebrities may have been paid to praise a product they tweet about.

If you use Twitter, keep in mind that while the laws about it are still evolving, there have been successful prosecutions for libel. Be a little cautious about what you type because what you 'post' is traceable.

Internet protection

Think of the story of the Trojan Horse – this is how computer viruses work. They pretend to be friendly but they will attack your computer, so installing anti-virus software is essential. Viruses enter your computer through files given to you, or most often via attachments to emails such as pictures or documents.

To protect against theft of your personal identity and information, you must install a 'firewall' piece of software. Anti-virus software and a firewall will protect your computer and your information, but need to be updated frequently. All-encompassing protection can be purchased from companies such as Norton or McAfee (there are many others), either in disk form or downloaded directly from their retail sites.

Scams

This is all exciting stuff, and if I've half converted you to join the technical revolution I don't want to put you off now, but I must point out that not all information technology is good because it has brought with it the risk of online fraud. This used to be considered the realm of sad geeks in back bedrooms, but now international gangs are at work and, for example, your credit card details may be for sale somewhere for less than a pound.

Most of the scams are fairly obvious. If you really think the new love you've found online is desperate to meet you but just needs help with the air fare … well, please give my regards to Santa Claus and the Tooth Fairy when you next see them. In reality, the more dangerous websites are set up to look like existing ones, whether banks or sales outlets for concerts and major sporting events, or fake sites springing up for donations when there is a world disaster.

Never send your bank account details to such sites and be equally cautious about opening suspicious emails; some may even falsely appear to have come from people you know.

And take the same care with computer passwords as you would or should with PIN numbers.

Think of the story of the Trojan Horse – this is how computer viruses work. They pretend to be friendly but they will attack your computer.

Final computer points

Many good things have stemmed from the computer explosion. To take just a few examples:

- Improved health care. This can range from simply being able to order repeat prescriptions online, to remote testing, feeding information to a doctor or nurse who can monitor your progress.

- There is less need to feel isolated as technology helps people keep in touch with friends and relatives. For example, with a webcam you can see the people to whom you are talking, which can be useful for relatives: it is less easy for an elderly person to bravely maintain 'I'm fine' if people can clearly see that they are not.

- Working from home may be possible, perhaps as you segue into retirement.

- Electronic book readers can hold thousands of books, weigh less than a paperback and even play music as you read. Some will magnify text to make it easier to read or convert text to speech so that you can listen to the book being read to you.

- Technology, then, can be awesome and far-reaching, although it is not all good news. Remember:

  - Information overload can create anxiety.
  - Too much time spent on the computer can lead to health problems, not least with your back and arms, and even repetitive strain injury (RSI). Take a break regularly.
  - Computer games may hinder young persons' communication skills. And the prolonged use of violent games can become addictive and may blur reality.

Whatever, computer technology is here to stay and, who knows, future generations may well have bar codes tattooed on their arms at birth. We used to say 'goo, goo' to babies; now people say 'Google, Google'.

Let's now look at some aspects of other communication technology in a little detail, with one important caveat: you do not have to have any of it. It is not compulsory. Not yet anyway.

Mobile phones

Like landline units, mobile phones are available hearing aid compatible and with big numbers and loud ringing tones. They are not just for talking into but are also used for texting, or SMS messaging to give it its official title. This was introduced as a way to send text messages from one mobile to another in the days before mobiles could send emails. The younger generation have for a long time had 'text speak', using abbreviated text such as LOL, either meaning Laugh Out Loud or Lots of Love. But why should youngsters have all the best abbreviations? There is perhaps a need for an STC (Senior Texting Code):

- ATD At the doctors.
- BYOT Bring your own teeth.
- FWIW Forgot where I was.
- ROFL–CGU Rolling on the floor laughing – can't get up.

Smartphones

These are effectively pocket-sized computers. In addition to making calls and sending text messages they can connect to the internet, allowing you to collect and send emails and surf the net. They can often double up as a camera or video recorder, a portable media player and a Personal Digital Assistant (PDA), keeping note of appointments and things to do. Many also incorporate GPS navigation, allowing you to display your location on a map and send it to a friend – useful if you are trying to meet someone and you are at one entrance to a shopping mall, while they are at another.

What really distinguishes Smartphones from the rest is their ability to download and run computer programmes (called applications or 'apps') which can do anything from helping you to follow a diet, translate foreign words and keep in touch with sports results, to working out where and when the sun will shine – a must for keen photographers and druids.

A Wi-Fi connection means you can surf the internet, download apps and send and receive emails at no cost and without using up credits on your phone. But where you see the Wi-Fi sign do check that the service is, in fact, free because some hotels, in particular, charge exorbitant rates for connections.

Once a year switch off all your personal communication gadgets for 24 hours. Guess what? An amazing thing will happen – the world will still go on.

Bluetooth

Like Wi-Fi, Bluetooth allows electronic equipment like mobile phones to communicate wirelessly. However, while Wi-Fi networks are publicly accessible and operate at all times, Bluetooth is designed to create a temporary network between a limited number of people and devices which have to be 'paired' before a connection can be made. You could use Bluetooth to send details of an event from your Smartphone's calendar to the mobile of a friend in the same room. (I knew I'd finally get you excited about the technology.)

Bluetooth is also used to connect hands-free earpieces and headsets to mobile phones.

Some of the up-to-date mobile phones that have internet connection may have the ability to scan bar codes and look for price comparisons. In this connection, the squiggly squares appearing in adverts and elsewhere are not examples of modern pop art but QR (Quick Response) codes which work in a similar way to a bar code. If you have an application on your mobile to scan the QR it will take you straight to a website and, for instance, a QR on a 'For Sale' board outside a house could take you to full brochure details.

iPads

Moving up from mobile phones, tablet PCs (e.g. iPads) sit between Smartphones and desktop computers. They use a touch screen instead of a physical keyboard and, while some use Windows operating systems, as found on PCs, most use systems like those developed for Smartphones so run apps rather than traditional software.

Final points

- If you are still not convinced and say 'I'll never use a computer', well, you'll have to throw away the microwave, the washing machine and countless other things you already use that depend on computers – including cars, of course.

- Don't be in awe of technology. In Stratford-upon-Avon I heard someone outside the Bard's birthplace huskily say: 'But think what Shakespeare would have done if he'd had a computer.' I know exactly what he would have done. He would have forgotten to save Macbeth and would have had the Merry Wives running a dodgy online escort agency, while Troilus and Cressida wouldn't have got through a spell check.

- All this technology can become addictive, so try an experiment. Once a year switch off all your personal communication gadgets for 24 hours. Guess what? An amazing thing will happen – the world will still go on.

'Why can't you play with your mobile phone like any normal person?'

STATE OF MIND

Don't be ashamed of growing old. People do it all the time. You will inevitably grow old, but you don't have to *think* old – and although some people are quite happy to retire mentally, a more positive approach may lead to a longer, happier life. 'Use it or lose it' is a cliché but, like many clichés, there is some truth in it – provided you can actually find 'it' in the first place, of course.

To remain alert, and to stress a point made earlier, always have a reason for getting out of bed in the morning. It has been said that you should know your limitations … and then ignore them. Well, maybe, but it is certainly good to have ambitions because life in the fast lane should mean more than just using the 'eight items or less' checkouts in supermarkets. But they should be realistic ambitions. Perhaps it's a bit late for swimming the Atlantic?

Doing good works has been found to be more beneficial than fun activities. Perhaps the human race is not as bad as we sometimes think.

Sense of humour

There are happy types and there are grumpy types. Which type you are may be due to your genes and just a fact of life, but surely it's better, if possible, to regard the bottle as half full not half empty? Laughing, happy people lead fuller lives, although statistically they don't necessarily live longer – perhaps because, as optimists, they take more risks.

Laughter cheers you up and a good belly laugh can even improve blood flow, release feel-good endorphins and ease tension. Constantly moaning and being bitter can make your health worse.

You don't stop laughing because you grow old. You grow old because you stop laughing. And let's face it, many areas of growing old can be funny, sometimes unexpectedly so – for example, a friend who uses a wheelchair was talking in a school about how youngsters should relate to the disabled. During the question session, one teenager asked 'What about sex?' The embarrassed gasp among the audience at his question turned into delighted laughter at her answer: 'It's not a problem … provided the brakes hold on the wheelchair.'

Below: The author's stepmother, Jill Summers, seen here on Margaret Thatcher's immediate right, appeared in *Coronation Street* well into her 80s. At her funeral Roy Barraclough – seen here behind the bar – recalled visiting Jill in hospital to find 15 people round her bed, all helpless with laughter at her humour, and all beneath a sign saying 'only 3 visitors at a time'.

Laughter cheers you up and a good belly laugh can even improve blood flow, release feel-good endorphins and ease tension.

If you are not already a subscriber, *The Oldie* magazine has a nicely wry approach to ageing, while if you can afford it the best medicine for gloom is to go to the Edinburgh Fringe and see a bunch of comedy shows. The audiences are all ages and the old don't feel out of place.

Stress

A bit of stress and pressure may be no bad thing and can be stimulating. But it is important not to get into a vicious circle where anxiety affects what you do and thus creates more anxiety.

Symptoms of stress include increased heart rate, blood pressure and breathing rate. You are likely to suffer from poor sleep patterns and be more inclined to smoke. And you get a dry mouth and sweaty palms, just as you do when you notice a blue light flashing in your rear view mirror when driving. Stress can produce tiredness and anxiety and, more seriously, 90% of suicides are people with mental stress.

Being told to 'snap out of it' or 'pull yourself together' won't help, and neither will exhortations to cheer up, unless you resolve what is actually causing your unhappiness.

Good ways to deal with stress include:

- Sorting out your affairs. This may help combat stress, for instance by leading you to seek help if you have money worries. And talk about things. People who have been through stressful times have told me they thought their feelings were best not shared because 'no one will understand'. Fortunately, they then realised they were wrong.

- Don't put off unpleasant tasks. They won't go away and that may become a cause of stress. It is tempting when opening mail or emails to deal with the nice and easy ones first. Try starting with the tough ones.

- Plan. It's only a four-letter word, but it can be a big help in countering stress. Reduce the stress of traffic by avoiding peak periods, for instance – one advantage of being retired is that you may be able to travel at different times. Planning may also help reduce the stress often caused by holidays.

- Don't fight what you can't alter. Global warming? The world coming to an end? Can you do anything about such things? No! So stop worrying about them.

- Relaxed, deep breathing may help combat stress, as can gentle and calming music. They both slow the pulse and the heart rate (so it was perhaps a mistake to put your Sinatra records on eBay).

- Lighting can play a significant part in influencing your mood. Even a new coat of paint using cheerful colours may help.

- Don't turn to booze; water will be better for you.

- If you usually take quick showers, try enjoying a long, leisurely bath with a book instead.

- Reading self-help books by people who have experienced similar problems to you may help. Some libraries have special sections of them.

- Even something as simple as birdsong can cheer you up, so put out the bread crumbs.

Anger

- Although research suggests that people are actually happier in their 70s and 80s because they have fewer responsibilities, plus the comfort of 'having seen it all before', the old are often viewed as bad-tempered and irascible. And of course many of us are. You might care to belie that impression.

- Anger can be a perfectly normal and healthy reaction to feeling threatened or frustrated. But anger stops being normal or healthy if it leads to major rows with friends or relatives, anti-social behaviour or even just a grumpy view of life.

Prolonged anger can be bad for your health, causing headaches, high blood pressure and even heart attacks or strokes. Best avoided, then…

- Prolonged anger can be bad for your health, causing headaches, high blood pressure and even heart attacks or strokes. Best avoided, then…

- Anger may be caused by something as basic as being on a diet, while if it is caused by failing to meet your retirement expectations … are they perhaps set too high?

- If there's something that causes you ongoing annoyance, try to resolve it rather than letting it fester. A dispute with a neighbour? Suggest a meeting over a coffee or something stronger. Irritated by some local rule or regulation? Try to do something about it via an action group.

- Exercise may help reduce anger because physical activity burns up stress hormones and boosts production of 'good mood' ones. Having a swear box, and perhaps giving the proceeds to charity, may help as well.

- If you are facing someone who is angry – perhaps when helping to herd recalcitrant spectators at an event – a friendly approach may work better than marching up, arms folded, with a 'what the hell do you think you're doing?' attitude.

Loneliness

Loneliness is rated by some as being as great a threat to health as smoking or being overweight, and it is an increasing issue as around half of those over 75 live alone.

Loneliness may be linked to depression and may make you more likely to drink too much, eat a poor diet and take little or no exercise.

To some extent loneliness may be an integral part of ageing – you lose friends as they die, maybe relatives move away and you no longer have the camaraderie of the workplace.

Loneliness is not a pleasant state. I'm sorry to labour the point if you winced at the last chapter on technology, but going online is a useful way of keeping in touch with people, although it can make things worse if it feels as if the whole world except you is having a great time. Face-to-face contact is better, so do try to get out and about, join clubs or volunteer and, above all, meet people and make friends. If you are naturally shy, try to find someone to go with you (organisers of events could help newcomers feel more at ease by wearing name badges). But you have to make the effort. You can't get a cure on the NHS. It has to be a DIY job.

'I'll only give you the paper if you promise not to let the news upset you.'

Depression

Depression is more than the perfectly normal sadness when something bad happens. Not simply a case of feeling a bit down in the dumps, depression can be much more serious and long lasting. It's a pretty common illness at any age, and should never be ignored as it can be treated.

Symptoms of depressive illness include difficulty getting to sleep, early morning wakening, being tired all the time, loss of appetite and loss of interest in things you normally enjoy.

These are not problems in isolation, but put them together over a sustained period and they can add up to an illness. You can overcome normal sadness given time, but with full-blown depression you can't without psychiatric help. In extreme cases depression can make people suicidal.

If you are depressed, you are not alone.

Prescriptions in the UK for anti-depressant drugs have shot up in recent years.

Beware of just struggling on with a stiff upper lip. A good cry may help. Don't bottle things up – if you're suffering from depression then talk about it, for instance by seeking help from your doctor if your health is your main worry. Depression is an illness not a crime. There is no stigma and the more things are discussed openly the better.

Something as simple as a brisk walk may help. Researchers in New York equipped 1,000 people with monitors and found that the more active people were, the lower their levels of symptoms of depression. Cheerful music may also help lift depression, although do consider the neighbours. And finally, women are more likely to become depressed than men. They may feel that this is because they have to deal with men. I couldn't possibly comment.

Symptoms of depressive illness include difficulty getting to sleep, early morning wakening, being tired all the time and loss of appetite.

Dementia & Alzheimer's

The number one concern people have about growing old is memory loss and the dreaded 'A' word – Alzheimer's – hence this stand-alone chapter before moving on to more general health matters.

First, if you forgot where your keys were a moment ago, don't go into panic mode because everyone forgets things from time to time. Make a joke of it. Your memory not being as good as it used to be is quite normal as you get older and people adjust – repeating people's names when you meet them may help you remember them, for instance. And don't use the random number given to you for a PIN, but use instead a number or word (preferably a combination) that means something to you personally so that you can work out what it is. If things become more serious then it may be that dementia is kicking in.

There is some confusion about dementia and Alzheimer's. The simplest way of thinking about dementia is that it is progressive 'brain failure'. This most commonly starts as memory loss, particularly loss of recent memory. But as the illness progresses, other problems can occur such as being unable to dress oneself. It's not that you can't *physically* perform each of the tasks required, but that you can't process how to do the whole thing – deciding which way up garments go, what order you put them on in and so forth. In the final stages, all learned behaviours are lost, e.g. feeding oneself, walking, talking, continence, etc.

In 1907 Alois Alzheimer, a German psychiatrist, described the commonest form of dementia, which was named after him. The second most common type is vascular dementia (also called multi-infarct dementia). There are other less common types as well. In life, it is often not possible to be sure of the cause of an individual's dementia – the only certain diagnosis comes after death if scientists do an autopsy and examine the brain under the microscope. There are some differences in the way dementia presents, progresses and is treated between the different types, but that is beyond the scope of this book. For the most part, which type of dementia someone has is of little relevance to the sufferers or their carers because all follow roughly the same path and cause the same difficulties.

The early symptoms may be varied. They will largely consist of memory loss, but could also take the form of repeated odd behaviours. It can kick in at any age, but the older you become, the greater the prevalence; 1 in 3 of over 65s may develop some form of dementia. There are more women with dementia than men, but this is because women live longer; men are likely to die of something else before they suffer dementia. There has been some suggestion that measuring testosterone levels may be a guide to dementing male patients, but not all doctors will be prepared to put demented old men on testosterone pills because their behaviour may be difficult enough without making them randy as well.

There are various scales to assess severity and it can be surprising how highly some people can score when no one in their family had any idea they even had a problem. The ability to remember the words of old music hall songs seems long lasting, however. I relished the time when a young doctor gave an elderly relative of mine, who had spent her life on the stage, six facts and said he would test her on them after giving her a medical examination … at which point my relative could remember all six, the doctor only four.

Despite suggestions that there should be mass screening for everyone over 60, some experts consider this misguided, believing you should only screen for something that you can treat successfully at an early stage (like cervical cancer); there are no early treatments for dementia. There is a push for earlier detection, that is investigation of people who have started to notice a problem but might otherwise have ignored it, and this does have some benefits. Control of vascular risk factors, for instance, may slow progression in someone with vascular dementia. Another benefit of earlier detection is being able get in touch with support services and to plan your own finances, future care and so on while you still have the mental capacity to do so – by the time the Mental Capacity Act becomes relevant it will be too late if you've demented beyond the point of being able to make your own decisions. But, against this, you then just

The early symptoms may be varied. They will largely consist of memory loss, but could also take the form of repeated odd behaviours.

Drugs have their place for some people but not all, and should not in any case be seen as a 'magic cure' – they're not.

know for sure that you're going to 'lose your mind' sooner than you would otherwise have been forced to acknowledge. And the system can't even look after the people with known dementia properly, hence the mixed feelings about pushing people to be checked out too soon.

Dementia care has been under-resourced, partly because people with dementia can't campaign themselves, and their carers are often too exhausted to fundraise although there are welcome signs that things are improving. Incidentally, both the Alzheimer's Society and Alzheimer's Research UK are excellent organisations for sufferers and their carers.

While there is perhaps no firm proof that being fit, mentally active, a non-smoker, of normal weight and with alcohol consumption under control actually helps, none of them can do any harm – and you'll feel better anyway, even if they don't stave off dementia.

High blood pressure and cholesterol in middle age may increase the risk, but only in the sense that these are vascular risk factors so can increase vascular dementia; but as they also increase the risk of heart attack and stroke you're more likely to die before you're old enough to dement.

If symptoms should start, don't go rushing off to live in the sun. There will be no benefit in going overseas – in fact, moving away from familiar surroundings is likely to expose the sufferer to greater problems.

Drugs have their place for some people but

'Remind me – am I getting up or going to bed?'

Who knows, in future years it may be possible to take a number of drugs to fend off the onset of Alzheimer's, just as we take statins now to prevent heart disease.

not all, and should not in any case be seen as a 'magic cure' – they're not. At best, they slow progression of the disease for a few years. Weird and wonderful oddball remedies are unlikely to be successful either, and taking an internet printout about one to the doctor will not be helpful. Taking a relative or friend who can describe what's been happening to you will be beneficial, however. And if a person can attend alone and give their doctor

a clear and full account of their concerns, almost by definition they don't have dementia.

The decline varies a lot both in speed and in which problems predominate in individuals, but the ultimate outcome will be very similar. People may completely recover from relapses with some illnesses, but in dementia cognitive function rarely improves. People with dementia are more prone to delirium, and they can improve from this, but often

not back to how they were before. Some sufferers report improvement when they start taking drugs, but most of the evidence suggests this is a placebo effect, or perhaps the optimism displayed by carers that something is being done makes the sufferer feel it must be helping. In general, drugs only stop you getting worse for a while rather than improving anything.

So I am sorry, but once it's lost it's gone for good. There may be no complete cure (as yet) but do bear in mind that we're talking here about overall function – people with dementia vary from day to day, sometimes from hour to hour. And it may not be all bad news: at a dementia group I attended one lady commented that her husband had become much nicer to live with since he'd been diagnosed with Alzimer's!

Who knows, in future years it may be possible to take a number of drugs to fend off the onset of Alzheimer's, just as we take statins now to prevent heart disease. Hopefully better treatments might emerge.

Dementia is not physically painful, but it is emotionally so when you know something is wrong but aren't sure what. Your hair doesn't fall out but you may fall over more frequently, because you can't process the muscle sequences required to walk safely and you might forget to take that stick or Zimmer frame that you need. Sufferers seem to lose language skills in reverse order of acquisition; those who spoke fluent English for many years but had a different mother tongue seem to lose their English skills but are still able to communicate in their first language.

Memory boxes may help, while in some areas there are memory cafes with, say, monthly meetings for those with problems. These can help because it is possible to share experiences with people who understand, and they are also places where sufferers can go to do a normal thing like have a coffee with friends. No one there will get upset if someone gets up and wanders off mid-conversation or otherwise behaves oddly – behaviour that might cause problems in 'normal' social situations.

You can get memo recorder/players that can help by playing recorded voice messages at programmed times, e.g. to remind you to take tablets or have something to eat, although these may have limited use.

Dementia doesn't cause any other physical illnesses, but sufferers may become violent and depressed, or happy and experience every other emotion known to man – often all at various times in the same person. This can make caring for Alzheimer's sufferers quite difficult (see the chapter on being a carer). There are lots of horror stories about poor care, but do remember that bad news sells newspapers and the countless examples of good care are rarely mentioned

The best thing going for sufferers is that people now talk about dementia openly, which removes the stigma there used to be: affected relatives are no longer being hidden in attics.

Parkinson's disease

Many people possibly confuse Alzheimer's and Parkinson's disease. There is a type of dementia – called Lewy body dementia – that people with Parkinson's get, but other than that there is no link at all. Parkinson's is a physical illness; the Lewy body dementia behaves (from the patient and carer perspective anyway) very much like any other form of dementia.

Perhaps one of the reasons why people get confused is that Parkinson's can affect your speech, which becomes quiet and indistinct, and you lose facial expression, which can be mistaken for cognitive impairment; it's not. In the same way, people who are very deaf can sometimes be labelled as confused. They don't hear what you say, but instead of saying so, they guess at what might have been said, get it wrong and come across as mentally impaired.

Parkinson's is a progressive degenerative disorder of the central nervous system with no known cause. The most obvious symptoms are related to movement – shaking, difficulty with walking and so on. It is rare before 40, but can physically become apparent at around 60. Dementia often occurs when Parkinson's is in the advanced stages.

Parkinson's is a progressive degenerative disorder of the central nervous system with no known cause. The most obvious symptoms are related to movement.

PHYSICAL HEALTH

Accept that age may bring its problems. You wouldn't expect a car to run for ever without problems, and you shouldn't expect your body to do so either. Just as you'd watch for rust spots on a classic car, watch for changes to your own classic bodywork too, like an unusual skin rash or a change in the appearance of a mole. And to continue the car comparison, just as you'd take one in for a service if it started misfiring, watch for personal changes too, such as a sudden shortness of breath, changes in your toilet habits, unusual bleeding or swellings. They could all be early warning signs of something serious and worth checking.

As is stressed throughout this book, your lifestyle can play a major part in your physical health, while not smoking, taking regular exercise, and the way you approach problems and get them fixed can also affect how long and healthily you live. A key person in the process is, of course, your doctor.

Getting the best from your doctor

● Try to develop a good relationship with your GP. This will help build trust and confidence in the treatment you receive.

'Which do you want to hear first? My attempt at humour, or the test results?'

● Keep appointments and be on time. Take reading material if you think you may have to wait as this might save you getting depressed looking at the notices and old magazines in the reception area.

● Don't waste your doctor's time. If you are bleeding from your bottom, say so; don't mention it as an embarrassed 'by the way' comment as you are leaving. Embarrassment can be a killer.

● If you have more than one thing to discuss, make a list to give to your doctor – this will help him or her to prioritise. It won't matter if it is scribbled on the back of a shopping list (unless, of course, the list is just for cigarettes and high-fat foods).

● There are websites which may help you understand more about your problems, but don't confront your GP with 37 pages pulled off the internet. The advantage of the internet is the volume of information available; its disadvantage is the volume of information available. Not all the information will be reliable and do remember that medical practices may be different in other countries.

Google 'headaches' and you'll get around 70 million hits. If you've got time to browse through those for gems for your GP then you really should get a hobby. Google medical matters enough and if you weren't a hypochondriac at the start you soon will be. (I looked up 'paranoid' and found it defined it as 'anyone who looks up "paranoid".')

● I know it's difficult if you have an ongoing ailment, but try not to let it dominate your every waking hour. If it is the only thing you ever talk about you may find yourself talking to yourself as friends edge away. It is very easy to become a hypochondriac, as my GP often hints. The malady lingers on.

● Remember that excellent information is available from charities involved with almost all ailments. Read such information so that you don't have to waste time asking your GP obvious questions.

● If you have a particular condition, such as diabetes or epilepsy, carry a card or disc to alert people who may be treating you in an emergency.

If you have a particular condition, such as diabetes or epilepsy, carry a card or disc to alert people who may be treating you in an emergency.

- Some newspapers give endless coverage to medical matters, sometimes citing esoteric research done on very small groups in distant countries. Such coverage may alarm you but, fortunately, there is a proven medical cure: change your newspaper.

- Don't get obsessed about reading the leaflets enclosed with any tablets you are given. The list of possible side-effects may be so exhaustive that you'll probably find you have some of them ... not necessarily due to the tablets. Leaflets are also not good at reminding you why you are on a tablet in the first place. Establish if there are any restrictions on how to take pills, e.g. before or after food, can you have a drink, etc., but only look at the small print if you experience a new symptom that you think might be related to the tablets.

- You can get pill boxes to cope with endless permutations, from one tablet a day to taking a variety of drugs at different times. Using a box will help ensure you take the right ones at the right time (some have alarm timers to remind you). Apart from anything else, it's more convenient to load such a piece of kit once a week rather than open umpteen tablet packets every day. But they are not for everyone. Some tablets should not be stored in a pill box for a prolonged period anyway, because they take in moisture from the air – that's why they come in blister packs from the manufacturer.
  If you take a self-filled box into hospital with you, it's important that there is a note on it saying what the tablets are (ideally the label off the box) because there are an awful lot of 'little white ones'! There are various compliance aids which all have their uses in different circumstances ... but again, one size does not fit all.

- Review your medicines with your GP or pharmacist at intervals. Some may have become unnecessary, others may not be wise in combination with other drugs, although hopefully the last point should not arise – it is the doctor's job to know about interactions when prescribing something new. However, they do need an accurate list of what you are on and, importantly, anything like herbal preparations you are buying from a chemist, a Chinese medicine store, a health food shop, or whatever. Some over-the-counter stuff will interact, so doctors need to know you are taking it.

- Dispose of tables safely when they are past their use-by date, ideally by taking them back to the pharmacy.

- You can ask to see your medical records, but be warned – a friend was alarmed to see 'NFR' written on his, thinking it stood for 'Not For Resuscitation'. He was only mildly relieved to be told that it meant 'Normal For Romford'.

- While doing all you can to help your GP to help you, there may come a time to put your foot down or, if the pain means you can't actually put it down, then bang on the desk instead to ask for more treatment. Old age should not be a reason to tolerate a constant nagging ache. And you are not being unreasonable if, after having had a specialist check, you ask what the results were. Ask the specialist about this, not the GP, although you may later need your doctor to explain some of the specialist's jargon. Remember that in fighting for your rights you are likely to obtain a better result if you adopt a calm rather than a combative approach.

- Be pleasant and courteous to reception staff and thank them if they have been helpful. A lot of the time they receive only negative feedback. And don't be two-faced – rude to the staff and sweet as pie to the doctors.

- If your GP has a 'Suggestion Box', use it – even if just to suggest that the practice should only supply soft (and therefore silent) toys for waiting children to play with, or that 'Another one bites the dust' is not exactly soothing music for the waiting room. More seriously, if the practice is lobbying against some local lunacy then consider supporting the campaign. And help in any trials or surveys too, because they may be important in developing cures.

Alternative remedies

- You can find pills or potions for everything, just as you can find alternative ways of treating things (sometimes very alternative). Before spending time or money on any of these, take a hard look at any background information. And don't hold out false hopes, because tests have shown that the vast majority offer nothing more than a placebo effect.

- As mentioned earlier, it is essential to tell your GP if you decide to try something different. 'Natural' does not necessary mean safe and something you decide to try may not react well with a medicine you are already taking. Some Chinese medicines, in particular, can be highly toxic.

- Whether alternative or mainstream, be cautious in buying cheap versions of drugs that may not have the effect of branded ones, and be very cautious about buying remedies online. The possibilities for counterfeit and perhaps dangerous pills are endless and obvious, and it is reckoned that half the medicines sold online are fakes. A warning sign is if an online site is prepared to sell you something without the slightest check on whether it is right for your condition. And which sounds more sensible: an online consultation with a doctor who has never met you or your usual GP? No contest, is there? If you still decide to go ahead with an online consultation, ensure that the doctor you are dealing with is registered with the General Medical Council.

- Keep in mind that, as banks and building societies constantly find, it is very easy to create a fake but official-looking online site. Some of the rip-offs will make your hair stand on end, while if you haven't got any hair you'll probably find tablets for sale online which guarantee to give you some. No!

- You will rarely be saving money buying online, so maybe it is embarrassment making you think of doing so; Viagra is perhaps the most common example. But don't be embarrassed about talking to doctors about such things – there is nothing they won't have heard before.

Treatment abroad

You can pay for medical and dental treatment abroad and, as the enticing leaflets often say, 'combine the treatment with a holiday in the sun'. Well, a holiday in the sun may not be exactly what you most want when undergoing treatment and you read too many horror stories to advise flying off for actual treatment for an illness without a great deal of checking first.

Specifics

After that broad introduction to physical health, let us now look at some specific conditions in a little more detail. This is not intended to be a medical encyclopaedia, but a totally unscientific survey of friends and relatives has indicated that the following are the things that cause most concern as people age. After dementia, which has already been covered in the previous chapter, the major concern is cancer.

Cancer

It's a chilling word. Cancer is high on most people's lists of fears. More middle-aged people are diagnosed with it than ever before, although some of the increase may be due to better screening methods. On a more positive note, lung cancer rates have fallen as people have stopped smoking, although the battle is not yet fully won.

But just what is cancer? Well, all body cells are renewed throughout your life – in simple terms, new cells replace old, worn-out ones – but the basic problem in all cancers is that abnormal new cells are formed, and keep forming; the normal 'new for old' substitution breaks down. You can't 'catch' cancer, by the way, so obviously there is no risk to carers.

It is not one disease: there are over 200 different types. So the first important question is, cancer of what? The answer has a huge impact on how serious the condition is and what treatments may be needed. Leukaemia, for instance, is a cancer of the blood-forming cells, so instead of the excess abnormal cells showing up as a lump, there are simply lots seen in the bloodstream.

Most but by no means all cancers are commoner

You will rarely be saving money buying online, so maybe it is embarrassment making you think of doing so; Viagra is perhaps the most common example.

Watch for odd skin changes and, in particular, for changes to any moles you have. Yes, a tan looks glamorous but acquiring one often simply isn't worth the risk.

....

as you grow older, with most cases occurring in the over 60s. Obviously some just occur in one sex – ovarian cancer only in women, prostate only in men. Breast cancer is commoner in women, but men can get it too.

The only certain tips for avoiding cancer are to remember the undisputed links between smoking and lung (and other) cancers, and between sunburn and melanoma. Links with obesity and alcohol are less definitive, but probably have some basis, albeit harder to 'prove'. Is it being fat that gives you cancer, or is it the junk food you eat (or lack of good food that you don't eat) that causes both the obesity and the cancer? However, being of normal weight, doing a bit of exercise and enjoying food and alcohol in moderation is always a good aim.

Diagnosis/symptoms

- Breast or testicular lumps or swellings that don't heal: visit your doctor fairly soon, as you should do if you have a cough for more than three weeks.

- Altered bowel habits, most commonly diarrhoea and/or bleeding, but any change which persists for a few weeks that is inexplicable by change of diet. (Ingest a load of stodge and don't be surprised when you get constipation; if you suddenly start eating tons of prunes, expect loose poo, verging on diarrhoea.) If a change in toilet habits comes out of the blue and persists for a few weeks, then get it checked.

    Over 35,000 people are diagnosed with bowel cancer in Britain every year and there is a high mortality rate – it is the UK's second biggest cancer killer – mostly because people ignore the warning signs, perhaps because of embarrassment. But we shouldn't be embarrassed because everyone defecates, even doctors, and most bowel cancers can be cured if caught in time.

    There is a simple NHS bowel cancer screening test which looks for blood in your stools. It simply involves collecting samples from your bowel movement and then posting them off for testing.

- Ovarian cancer has been dubbed 'the silent killer' because often a lack of clear symptoms means it's discovered too late. Ask for a test if you frequently feel bloated or become full quickly, even if eating less, or if you need to urinate urgently or frequently.

- Watch for odd skin changes and, in particular, for changes to any moles you have. Yes, a tan looks glamorous but acquiring one often simply isn't worth the risk. The sun is the key cause of skin cancer so avoid sunburn, which can double your risk. Cover up, wear a hat and use a good sunscreen. And keep out of the midday sun: it may be too strong no matter what precautions you take.

- Unexplained weight loss. You've eaten less and lost weight? Good for you, well done on the diet, but don't go to the doctor. But if you're eating as normal but the weight is dropping off, go to your doctor for tests (although there are non-cancerous possibilities as well). Also go if the reason you're eating less is due to symptoms of nausea, food sticking in your throat, etc.

- Go for screening – smears, mammograms, etc. – when invited, not because you've read some scare story in a newspaper. Screening programmes are carefully evaluated, but picking up something sooner when there's nothing that can be done about it is not a good thing; you will just suffer, knowing you've got cancer, for longer. There should only be screening when picking something up early leads to a treatment that can potentially cure.

- There are mixed views on the benefits of a PSA (Prostate-Specific Antigen) test for men. I've found it comforting to have one every couple of years, but that could be because the readings barely change. There is a medical view that a weekly orgasm or two may help 'to keep the pipes clear' and reduce the risk.

Treatment

Don't panic if cancer is diagnosed. A few days or even weeks for thought, and perhaps a second opinion, are not likely to exacerbate things.

There may be something of a postcode lottery regarding some treatments, and not all treatments will be available on the NHS because the extra benefits of using them can be quite hard to justify on economic grounds. It's not an easy debate, but are Y months of extra life (and not necessarily pain-free months) worth the extra £X spent on drugs?

The treatment for cancer depends on what cancer you have and whether it has spread at the time of diagnosis. If the cancer has not spread, there is a good chance that it might be curable. If it has spread outside the part of the body where it started to nearby structures (this is termed 'locally invasive'), but not gone to other parts of the body, treatment is likely to be more extensive, but there is often still a good chance of cure. Unfortunately, once it has spread to other parts of the body from where it started (the medical term for this is 'metastasised'), then a cure is no longer possible. In some cases, though, treatment will lead to remission or control of the disease for quite a long time, many years in some cases.

Treatments for cancer fall into three main categories: surgery, radiotherapy and chemotherapy. Surgery is self-explanatory – an operation to remove as much of the tumour as possible. Radiotherapy is radiation treatment given via external machines or implants directly inserted into the tumour. Chemotherapy is drug treatment, most commonly administered directly into the bloodstream via an injection or infusion, although some types are taken orally.

There are many different chemotherapy drugs and they are given in different combinations depending on the clinical circumstances. Chemotherapy is the treatment most commonly associated in people's minds with hair loss and sickness – both of these side-effects can occur with some drug combinations, but not all, while the sickness can usually be well controlled with other medications. Different treatments may be combined to maximise damage to the cancer cells and minimise damage to the surrounding normal cells.

It is important to follow any instructions you are given when being treated and it may help you cope if you learn something about your condition and ask questions, but don't become overly combative in the desperate desire to find a miracle cure. Not everyone wants to know everything, and it's not compulsory! Some people are happier knowing just enough to decide whether to have the suggested treatment but prefer to let doctors decide the rest.

Cancer is an emotive topic and sufferers understandably may become angry and/or frightened at their fate. But they will probably find plenty of support from friends, relatives and excellent charities. Cancer research is progressing every year. Survival rates continue to improve and half those diagnosed with cancer may live more than five years. And, yes, there is hope for the future with many research projects under way.

Cardiovascular risks

This may seem rather a technical title for this section, but not if you consider that 'cardiovascular' comes from 'cardio' = heart and 'vascular' = blood vessels. So this section covers heart, blood pressure and strokes because they are interlinked. And it's an important section, because cardiovascular disease, including coronary heart disease, stroke and some aspects of diabetes and kidney disease, affects the lives of over four million people in the UK.

Blood pressure

Blood pressure is a recording of the pressure of the flow of blood round the body. The top reading (= systolic blood pressure) is the peak pressure when the heart pulses and squeezes blood round the body; the lower reading (= diastolic blood pressure) is the pressure when the heart is in the relaxed phase of the cycle. So blood

Don't panic if cancer is diagnosed. A few days or even weeks for thought, and perhaps a second opinion, are not likely to exacerbate things.

pressure is recorded xxx/yy (e.g. 120/80) and the units are mmHg, that is millimetres of mercury.

High blood pressure is of concern because it puts the blood vessels at too high a pressure and causes damage – particularly in small blood vessels like those in the brain, the back of the eye and the kidneys. If not controlled, it is one of the major factors in strokes.

High blood pressure usually causes no symptoms at all in the vast majority of cases, so periodic checks are a good idea. Your GP will probably automatically test when you visit for other things. They should allow for 'white coat syndrome', the fact that people may be nervous simply because they are at the doctor's. A routine check may be followed by having a 24-hour monitor fitted.

People attribute various symptoms to their blood pressure – but they are usually mistaken. Low blood pressure (hypotension) can make you feel light-headed. Very high blood pressure (hypertension) might cause headaches – but headaches are common and high blood pressure is common – one is very rarely the actual cause of the other.

High blood pressure may be caused by obesity, excessive alcohol consumption, smoking, lack of exercise and diabetes. It can also be just bad luck, and you may be more likely to suffer from it if it has run in the family.

High blood pressure itself usually has no effect on daily living – you become ill or die from the heart attack or stroke. 'Detected early' isn't really relevant in this case because it's not like cancer. It can be treated just the same whenever it's diagnosed, but there is no total cure. Stopping smoking, losing weight and taking more exercise are all likely to help, although sufferers are still likely to need tablets eventually.

If untreated, the condition will steadily worsen, but just as some unrepentant smokers live long, healthy lives, so do some people with untreated hypertension. There are no absolutes. And as you get older the side-effects of treatment become more important.

At the other end of the scale, low blood pressure is mostly due to over-treatment of high blood pressure and is solved by simply stopping the drugs. Some people have lower than average blood pressure, but it's normal for them and not an issue. There are no symptoms if it's just your normal state.

'Postural hypotension' is relatively common in elderly folk. When you stand up your head is a couple of feet further away from the centre of the earth than it was when you were seated, so to counteract the pull of gravity your blood pressure should go up a little – this is normal. For various reasons, this reflex response can be a little delayed, meaning that when you stand up the blood pressure drops initially so you feel light-headed. This is a risk factor for falls. Often this is made worse by treatment for high blood pressure. If it affects you, say when you get up in the morning, sit on the edge of the bed for a moment or two before standing, then stand still before walking.

Low blood pressure is only as 'dangerous' as high blood pressure when you fall over and break something.

DVT

And while we are discussing blood, what about blood clots? They're now much less likely to occur in hospitals as they are policed very tightly on instituting preventative measures. When travelling, do the exercises they show you on the flight briefing – it's the calf muscle you need to move most, so toe wriggling is not enough. The flight socks that are sold can also be useful, with graded compression up the calf, but preventative measures only lower the risk – they can't abolish risk altogether and some may still be unlucky.

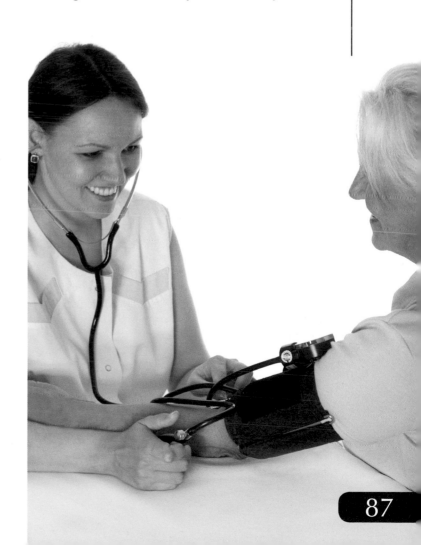

Now we come to the engine room. A failure there – a heart attack – is high on many people's list of concerns.

Cholesterol

There are no symptoms of high cholesterol, but it is a key constituent in hardening of the arteries. High levels of cholesterol in the blood are associated with a higher risk of coronary heart disease – the cholesterol itself is not life-threatening, but the heart attacks and strokes certainly are.

Treatment? Much the same as healthy eating guidelines – less fat, especially fats rich in saturates, and more fruit and vegetables. Don't overdose on sugar or salt. And try to take more exercise. Such measures are rarely effective alone, unless your diet was really terrible beforehand and you have the willpower to change completely, so drugs will usually be involved as they can bring most people's level down to within the normal range.

If you are diagnosed with high cholesterol – and the test involves simply having a sample of blood taken and tested – you will be given a recommended diet and plan of action. Follow it.

Heart

Now we come to the engine room. A failure there – a heart attack – is high on many people's list of concerns.

Just what is a heart attack? The basic disease process is that the arteries of the heart 'fur up' with something called atherosclerosis. At times, not enough blood gets through the narrowed artery, so the heart muscle supplied by that artery gives you pain – think of the calf muscle if you walk too fast up a hill. This heart pain is called angina. You stop and use your medication, enough blood gets through to supply the muscle, the pain goes and no permanent damage is done. During a heart attack (medical term: myocardial infarction) the blockage to the heart artery becomes complete and some or all of the heart muscles supplied by that artery are permanently damaged. The consequences of this can be anything from minor damage that you never knew had happened (it might be picked up later on a scan or heart tracing) right up to sudden death – it depends on which artery is blocked.

The symptoms of a heart attack are very variable and include chest pain (tight central chest pain, often radiating down the left arm and/or up into the jaw), feeling clammy, nausea and vomiting, breathlessness and sometimes palpitations. (Lay people tend to use the term 'heart attack' to mean all sorts of things, including angina and palpitations.) So … Chest pain? Short of breath? Feeling faint? If it's severe, don't wait for an appointment with a GP, dial 999 because time is all important.

To lessen your chances of having a heart attack:

● Don't smoke. This should be so obvious as not to need constantly repeating throughout the book, yet the sad sight of people puffing away outside offices and shops suggests the message is still being ignored.

● In general, exercise is good, but if you're suffering from heart disease it might bring on an attack that will kill you. However, gentle graded exercise is used after heart attacks to help the heart to open up smaller arteries naturally, to compensate for the narrowed bigger ones. To use a road analogy, if the M1 is permanently narrowed, encourage the A1 to widen.

● Reduce your weight.

● Don't overdose on alcohol, and don't use too much salt because it is one of the causes of high blood pressure.

● Getting very angry about something can be a trigger, in the same way that exertion can trigger an attack. Both stress and exertion cause your pulse and blood pressure to rise, which in turn means the heart muscle needs more oxygen to keep working faster and harder, so a narrowed artery is more of a problem (just as major roadworks cause traffic jams during rush hour but no delays at quieter times). But anger or exercise doesn't cause the heart disease in the first place; they just might bring an attack on sooner than would have happened naturally.

Heart attacks and treatment

If you see someone showing signs of having a heart attack, dial 999. You might try mouth-to-mouth breathing, to get air into the lungs: the 'kiss of life'. If you are concerned about transmittable disease, a plastic bag can easily be used as a shield … but don't dither too long because if someone's heart has stopped, the brain can only live for three to four minutes before death may result.

In hospital the emergency team may use a machine to give an electric shock, hence the 'stand back' scenes beloved of TV hospital dramas, but this is not a 100% cure – less than a fifth of patients who have received CPR (cardio-pulmonary resuscitation) live. It won't help everyone. Note in this context that you can refuse cardio-pulmonary resuscitation and, once informed, the medical staff must respect your wishes. This won't affect other treatment you may be receiving.

Lots of different drugs are used in treating heart problems. No drugs used to treat heart disease should cause a major panic if you accidentally miss a dose, but they do need to be taken as prescribed to be effective. If you are considering stopping one because you think it is causing side-effects, discuss this honestly with your doctor because alternatives may be available.

Having a pacemaker fitted is a relatively common procedure if your heart intermittently slows down too much – this can cause blackouts because if the heart goes too slowly the 'pump' does not get the blood up to the brain (like stalling a car). The pacemaker monitors the heart speed, and if it detects a slowing below a set threshold it takes over and delivers a steady electrical signal to the heart to make it beat at the right speed. Pacemakers are put in under local anaesthetic and can completely solve the problem. They can be a bit of an aggravation at airports, but otherwise users often lead normal lives.

This is an area where knowledge is advancing very quickly and you should take advice from doctors, who will be aware of the latest thinking. And do follow advice, for instance on walking so many yards or miles per day while recuperating.

The aim is always a return to normal life, but not everyone manages this. It is usually heart failure that causes permanent disability after heart attacks: if quite a lot of heart muscle has been permanently damaged the pump is not as strong as it was and this can cause fluid to build up around ankles and in the lungs.

To end this section on a lighter note … the Japanese eat very little fat and suffer fewer heart attacks than us; Mexicans eat a lot of fat and suffer fewer heart attacks than us; the Chinese drink very little red wine and suffer fewer heart attacks than us; Italians drink a lot of red wine and suffer fewer heart attacks than us; the Germans drink beer and eat lots of sausage and fats, and suffer fewer heart attacks than us; the French eat foie gras, full-fat cheese and drink red wine and suffer fewer heart attacks than us. The conclusion? Eat and drink what you like. It's speaking English that kills you.

Strokes

In effect, a stroke is a brain attack and is caused when the blood supply to part of the brain is disrupted. There are two main types – ischaemic (= blocked blood vessel) and haemorrhagic (= bleed).

Risk factors include high blood pressure, raised cholesterol levels, atrial fibrillation (irregularly irregular pulse), carotid artery stenosis (blockage of the main arteries that supply the brain) and diabetes (which adds additional risk factors to high blood pressure so sufferers are at a higher risk of stroke).

Heredity can play a part. You may be more at risk if a family member has had a stroke, but strokes are common so just because two close relatives suffer a stroke doesn't necessarily mean this is anything more than bad luck. Age also plays a part; the older you are, the more likely you are to have a stroke.

The media reports from time to time on research 'proving' or disproving that this or that drink or food item reduces or increases the risk of a stroke, but it is probably better to wait until the research finds its way into mainstream medicine before reacting or clutching at straws.

Use the FAST test (face–arm–speech–time), covered in Chapter 1, to recognise symptoms. The test is aimed at getting people to hospital quickly, where they may be suitable for thrombolysis (clot-busting drugs). Unfortunately, in the majority of cases, there's little to be done (though there are new treatments on the horizon) other than good basic care so that the patient doesn't die from a complication, e.g. pneumonia due to aspiration, as swallowing is commonly unsafe in the early phase.

Treatment mostly consists of managing and treating the complications, followed by rehabilitation using physiotherapy/occupational therapy/speech therapy, plus treating any risk factors to prevent another stroke. (If you've had one your chances of suffering another are higher.) Quite a lot of people do make a full recovery, but others may end up very disabled.

Although one person's symptoms may be similar to a friend's, their recovery may be very different. It may even depend on motivation, although this can be a tricky one – sometimes people do try very hard but get nowhere, while do-gooders saying 'positive mental attitude' are unhelpful as the patient becomes even more miserable thinking lack of progress is their own fault.

A stroke sufferer will almost certainly be offered support from a therapist to help with balance and walking; he or she, as well as social services, will also advise on what mobility aids may be needed and whether the home needs adapting, with ramps or handrails, for instance, to help with moving around.

The support of friends and relatives may be important as you adapt to the after-effects of a stroke and, for example, perhaps learn to use one arm not two when getting dressed. Joining a stroke club may help too, because you will be able to share experiences and take part in activities to help your recovery.

As well as physical effects, a stroke may also cause problems with speech, memory and vision. Treatment is available for all such conditions. Not surprisingly, depression may be a problem. Again, treatment is available.

Bear in mind that you are not allowed to drive for at least a month after a stroke. After this time you need to see your GP, who can advise whether you may start driving again. If you receive the go-ahead, you should notify your insurance company – if you don't then future claims may be rejected. If you are not cleared to drive after the month, you should contact the DVLA who will send you a questionnaire to complete. An assessment at a mobility centre may follow. Anxious though you may be to resume normal life after a stroke, driving is one area where a cautious approach is definitely advisable.

Finally, I know from personal experience, when a close relative had a stroke, just how helpful is the superb material available from the Stroke Association.

Hearing loss

Hearing problems are not life-threatening (unless you fail to hear that van coming), but they can be a major concern, not least for friends and relatives. Although my editor does not like me using italic type, I must use it here in order to stress that *hearing loss does not mean loss of brain power.* Treating the hard of hearing as if they are retarded, boring old f**ts is wrong and insulting.

Around 1 in 7 of adult Europeans suffer from hearing loss yet only 1 in 6 of them actually have aids fitted. It can take around seven years from starting to suffer hearing loss to finally admitting that you need aids and that the problem is not just that everyone around you is mumbling.

As regards causes of hearing loss, the biggest danger is noise – and loud noises in particular. If you are very unlucky, your hearing can be permanently damaged by one sudden loud noise, but more commonly there will be a slow and progressive deterioration. The effect of noise on hearing is well known, yet people persist in being in acoustically hostile environments without taking precautions (e.g. some work environments, spectating at motor events, listening to live or recorded music at too high a decibel level). The louder a noise, the shorter the time you can be exposed to it without damaging your ears.

As we grow older our hearing changes gradually, but some of us have a head start because of noise damage. Also, old and/or chronic ear infections and some hereditary causes of hearing loss can tip listening ability beyond the 'coping OK' level to the 'not managing too well' level, especially when in groups and with background noise.

The most common problem is not hearing the high frequencies so well and this means we cannot hear all the parts of speech correctly. We then mishear parts of what someone is saying and perhaps make a wrong guess. That's when it starts to become embarrassing. So do something about it and have a hearing assessment done.

Not everyone has the same type or degree of hearing loss, and therefore a proper assessment will show if it is significant, or if there is a medical or surgical solution. Sometimes, and mainly, there is

The most common problem is not hearing the high frequencies so well and this means we cannot hear all the parts of speech correctly.

It is very rare for a hearing loss to be so great that nothing can be done. Even the profoundly deaf try hearing aids first, before looking into implants.

no surgical solution and hearing aids are needed to improve your hearing. Don't leave it until you are a complete nuisance to others who, sad to say, quite often will say 'Don't worry, it doesn't matter' when asked for a repeat the second time around.

Tinnitus

This is the ringing, whistling or other odd sounds that people can hear inside their heads.

People with tinnitus don't necessarily have loss of hearing, but sufferers should not just bravely tolerate tinnitus; they should seek advice because it could be an early warning of more serious hearing problems. It can be caused by loud noise, or be the side-effect of some medication, or even triggered by emotional stress, and it can be very distressing and often impossible to treat.

Sufferers may find their tinnitus is better where there is a certain amount of background noise rather than dead silence. But although there is no cure, as such, tinnitus can be helped by audiologists with counselling, advice on diet and use of hearing aids or maskers to help sufferers adjust to the condition and learn to cope and keep it as a manageable state.

It is difficult, I know, but try not to think about it. As a (mild) sufferer I hadn't got tinnitus when I started typing this section but I have now. So, moving quickly on…

Signs of hearing loss

- The best indication is that family and friends will tell you.

- Try talking to people without looking at them. It is surprising how much we may rely on lip-reading.

- Turning your TV up higher than other viewers want.

- In noisy places like hamburger joints, getting 'edgy' at the background chatter, not the food. However, if you find yourself incensed by background music in restaurants this does not necessarily mean that you have hearing loss, just good taste.

Hearing tests

You can cope with hearing loss via subtitled films and TV, louder door bells and smoke alarms, special telephones and so on, and there is a huge range of special products available, but it is far better to take more positive action to address the problem by having a hearing test.

The government recommends a hearing test every year, just as for eyes, but few people seem to bother. Yet a test will only take 20 minutes or so and is very simple. You will be put in a soundproof booth to listen to sounds of different pitch and loudness. You have to press a button when you hear a sound. No injections are involved.

If you are lucky, a test may show that you have become hard of hearing simply because of a build-up of wax. Proper examination, with a good light or even a camera in the ear canal, will show any wax or other outer ear problem.

It is very rare for a hearing loss to be so great that nothing can be done. Even the profoundly deaf try hearing aids first, before looking into implants.

Hearing aids

Behind-the-ear hearing aids with ear moulds are becoming rather outmoded now, and the small behind-the-ear types with a wire to a loudspeaker in the ear are starting to become more readily available. The more sophisticated systems can be found in the private sector rather than the NHS, including ear aids which fit inside the canal and outer ear, although these can be visible.

Completely in-the-canal aids are very small and cosmetically appealing, but they can feel rather 'blocking' in the ear. (Some people prefer these to conceal the fact that they need hearing assistance. I don't see the point myself – there is no shame in having hearing loss.) Aids can be fixed on to spectacles, too, but if the glasses break and have to go away for repair, you cannot hear, while if the aid goes wrong you cannot see!

It is the number and level of sophistication of the features incorporated in the software which gives the edge, but not everyone needs a 'Rolls-Royce'. Those who just need to hear in simple listening environments can have less complex instruments. Different types of hearing aids suit different hearing losses and meet different lifestyle needs. Whatever the type:

● Consider insuring your aids. Dogs love to eat them, cats play with them and lawn mowers are regular chewers of hearing aids.

● Ensure they will be compatible with your phone.

● Expect a shock when you first wear them – what you think is a major tornado will probably be the audiologist's kettle boiling.

● Break them in gradually. Accept that it may take a little time to get the best out of them. If you have been endlessly putting off getting aids, your brain will take a little time to tune in.

● Let the specialist know if you are not hearing well with them.

● Get into a routine of looking after them.

● Don't get them wet. They can be so comfortable to wear that you may be tempted to plunge into a bath … still wearing them.

● Remove them before using hair spray, which could block the inlets.

● Ensure you have a loud or vibrating alarm clock because when you take your aids out before sleep the silence will be deep (and golden).

● Carry spare batteries because the bleeping to indicate failing power will invariably start when you are away from home.

● Keep your ears free of wax. Don't poke. Put nothing smaller than your elbow in your ear. But do get your ears looked at regularly as even a modest amount of wax can make hearing aids whistle. Ask your local NHS practice to help, or if your private audiologist is qualified then he can remove it.

● Finally, there will be very pleasant surprises in store if you start wearing hearing aids. Switch them off and they act as earplugs and can save you the torment of some of the more grating TV voices, while if you go to a theatre, church or other venue with a loop or infrared system you will find you will hear better than those around you. It almost feels as if the artists are sitting on your knee.

Diabetes

Diabetes occurs when the level of glucose in the body is too high because it is not being processed properly. It stops your system converting the sugars and starches in your body into energy. Some 2.5 million people in the UK have diabetes, while probably up to a million more have it but don't know they do.

There are two types:

● Type 1, which requires insulin from the start, is most likely to occur in childhood or adolescence so is not covered here.
● The far more common Type 2 is usually found in the over 40s (although it's now being diagnosed in younger people). It is preventable and occurs when the body doesn't produce enough insulin, or what it does produce doesn't work effectively. Dietary modification may be sufficient to control things in the earliest stages, then various different tablets can be prescribed. Some people do end up on insulin as the disease progresses, but by no means all.

www.naturalhearing.co.uk

You can't 'catch' diabetes. The big increase is due to the rise in obesity, but some people of normal weight get Type 2. This is just bad luck.

There are often no symptoms – doctors may pick it up as an incidental finding when doing a routine test as part of an investigation of an unrelated illness. A few patients will be diagnosed for the first time by their optician, who sees early changes on the retina and tells you to go to the doctor. People diagnosed in this way will be Type 2 diabetics and may have had the disease for years without knowing it. It is commonly said that people have Type 2 for about ten years before it comes to light. But signs can include:

● Frequently passing water.
● Often feeling thirsty.
● Always feeling lethargic.

Diabetes greatly increases the chances of a heart attack or stroke so it is worth seeking treatment. Although it can sometimes be controlled just by diet, there is no total cure. There are, however, lots of different options and several new treatments have come on the market in recent years – some tablet, some injection. Taking insulin is not inevitable, so don't postpone seeking help if you've got symptoms just because you're frightened of being told you'll need to inject yourself. Even that is nothing like as bad as people fear. It is all very simple these days: the needles are so small and fine that patients hardly notice them.

I've probably harped on more than enough about not smoking and maintaining a healthy diet, but this is essential in fighting and controlling diabetes. Avoid the usual suspects like salt and sugary or fatty foods (a US study found that eating bacon every day raised the risk of developing Type 2 diabetes by over 50%). Keep an eye on your cholesterol level and maintain a sensible weight and shape; 'central' obesity is generally thought to be the worst sort, with apple-shaped people more at risk than pear-shaped ones.

It follows that exercise will help in controlling diabetes, but check first with your GP that your condition is stable enough for you to start exercising and then, when you do, warm up before exercising and build up an exercise routine gradually.

Get well-fitting shoes for exercising, and check your feet regularly for any irregularities – one of the long-term complications of diabetes is damage to peripheral nerves so that sensation in your feet isn't as good as it was. You might develop ulcers and not even notice because you don't feel any pain.

Finally, diabetes can make you more likely to have problems with your gums, so brush regularly and well, and have regular dental checks.

Sex

It has been suggested that I should just put 'yes' here and then carry on to the next section, but the subject is more important than that. Lovemaking doesn't have to stop with age: a US study showed that 63% of men and 30% of women aged between 80 and 102 still have sex. The mind boggles.

It's good exercise anyway. Lovemaking three times a weeks burns the same calories as jogging for half an hour. And it doesn't do so much damage to your leg joints.

GOLDEN WEDDING

It was the sex that kept us together... we never had any

. GED

Create the right environment for sleep: a dark room (not too warm) without a lot of noise and with a comfortable bed.

Erectile dysfunction can be related to diabetes, medication, heart disease, smoking and alcohol; psychological problems are the cause in a lot of cases too. Viagra can be effective in appropriate subjects, but do have a medical check before using it, as it can be dangerous in some people. Never buy pills online (and don't believe claims for treatments to increase penis length by improbable amounts either).

A few men suffer from Peyronie's disease, which can result in the erect penis being bent, but this need not affect lovemaking … once you've both stopped laughing.

For women, the main 'mechanical' problem is vaginal dryness which causes discomfort; go to your GP with this because there are creams that help.

Talk to your partner about any concerns related to sex and remember that there doesn't have to be a 'target' of so many times a week. And don't believe any surveys on the subject, because it's one about which people lie (as they perhaps did in the US survey quoted above).

Never be embarrassed about talking to your GP. This particularly applies if you have had a heart attack, although the risk of sex triggering another one is small.

Try to maintain a sense of humour; sex can be slightly absurd at any age, not just when you are old. Put a lock on the bedroom door to avoid distressing your children and grandchildren, who may be alarmed to find that sex is still possible in retirement, draw the blinds if the window cleaner is due and, finally, remember that if it doesn't work out there is still much pleasure to be had from lying in bed together studying the latest seed catalogue. Or so I'm told.

Sleep

Perhaps it is appropriate that 'sleep' should follow the previous topic, although there is not a lot about sleep that is unique to older people. The elderly do tend to nap a lot, particularly when they are physically less able so they can't do as much … and then they complain that they can't sleep at night!

- If something is bothering you and likely to stop you sleeping, try to deal with it otherwise you may get the dreaded 4am blues. This is when you lie awake worrying about issues not just in your personal life but in the world as a whole. Regular early morning wakening can be a symptom of depression, i.e. an actual depressive illness, not just a transient thing that's worrying you.

- Create the right environment for sleep: a dark room (not too warm) without a lot of noise and with a comfortable bed.

- Don't overdo the alcohol as this will affect the number of loo breaks you need, especially in the latter part of your sleep. If you do get out of bed, don't put on bright lights because these may stop you getting back to sleep.

- A couple of the most energetic oldies I know swear blind by a half-hour nap after lunch every day.

- Some sleeping tablets can be addictive, although not all of them. If you take a sleeping tablet regularly and have been doing so for years, don't just stop them without checking with your GP first. Some have significant withdrawal problems if stopped abruptly.

Snoring

- Some 40% of us snore. The muscles relax in your mouth, nose and throat when you sleep which means the airways close up.

- Causes? Smoking, excessive alcohol and being overweight don't help, but these are obviously not specific to the elderly.

- A snorer may often be less affected than their partner. Excessive snoring can lead to tensions and even marital breakdowns.

- The plaster things athletes use on their noses can be effective as they hold the air passages open, while if all else fails earplugs are available from most good chemists.

Bladder and bowels

Although we all defecate and urinate on a regular basis, this is still a subject regarded with embarrassment – and perhaps the worst fear about growing old is having your bottom wiped, or an incontinence pad changed, by a relative or relative stranger.

Sufferers are not alone. It is estimated that 25% of the UK population have had problems with bladder control. It's not inevitable but it is very common, with lots of different causes. Faecal incontinence is much less common than urinary dysfunction, but does happen with increasing frequency with age.

The only connection between bladder and bowels is that both are evacuated in the toilet – there's a popular misconception that there's a link between the two processes, but this isn't true. About the only 'link' is that it's virtually impossible to have a poo without peeing at the same time, but this is about conventional toileting behaviour rather than any anatomical link. The only other connection is that constipation may well cause urinary retention (an inability to pee) purely because bowel loops full of poo press on the outflow pipe from the bladder as both lie in the pelvic cavity.

Bladder

Wetting yourself is not a normal part of getting old so, instead of buying expensive products in the supermarket, it's worth checking it out. A minor dribble when coughing or laughing is very common (it's called stress incontinence) and if it's minor, with perhaps a panty liner for reassurance, then you can probably ignore it. But if you suffer flooding with no warning or you are paying a fortune for pads then get yourself checked. Stress incontinence can cause more major problems; treatment can be quite difficult as the basic problem is weak pelvic floor muscles, meaning the bladder sphincter leaks.

The other main cause of incontinence is urge incontinence (or detrusor instability). The bladder wall is made of a muscle tissue which normally only contracts when the brain tells it that you are on the loo and it's OK to pee, but it can become irritable and contract without warning, leading to a sudden, urgent desire to pee, and often incontinence too, either because you can't get to the loo quickly enough or because you've also got stress incontinence and the sphincter isn't strong enough to 'hang on'. This type of incontinence can often be treated with medication.

The main message, though, is that incontinence is not inevitable. Chart what's happening for a few days before going to your doctor, note your fluid intake (type and volume), when you go to the loo, approximately how much you peed and, when incontinent, whether it was a dribble or a flood. All this information will help your GP to make a diagnosis. He or she may refer you to a specialist continence clinic.

An irritated bladder, often triggered by inflammation due to infection, the menopause, spicy foods and some drinks like coffee and alcohol, can lead to frequent trips to the loo and may also be painful. Painful peeing is most commonly due to infection – take a sample to your GP and get treatment if needed. Infection might temporarily cause incontinence because of irritation to the bladder (a bit like the urge incontinence described above). People sometimes reduce their fluid intake when this happens, because they are worried about making it to the loo in time, but this is not the right thing to do because the urine then becomes more concentrated and more likely to cause irritation.

Women are more prone to infections because their outflow pipe is shorter than a man's (it doesn't run down a penis) so bugs get in more easily. Stress incontinence occurs mostly in women too; urge incontinence affects both sexes. Pelvic floor exercises will help a woman with stress incontinence (doesn't do anything for urge) but people are notoriously bad at doing them so they often don't work. Men also have a pelvic floor apparently but because the anatomy is different exercising it won't help incontinence.

Prostrate problems in men can cause urinary retention. This can be partial, with incomplete emptying of the bladder, or sometimes complete blockage. You'd certainly know about the latter

It is estimated that 25% of the UK population have had problems with bladder control. It's not inevitable but it is very common, with lots of different causes.

pretty quickly as the very full bladder is painful and usually ends with a visit to A&E for a catheter to be put in as an emergency.

Have bladder problems treated, because they can affect your life – for instance, if you have to plan journeys according to where the loos are. I mentioned lobbying in an earlier chapter – a suitable case for action could be trying to stop local councils closing public loos to save pennies by stopping people spending pennies. It's crazy in tourist towns, in particular.

Incontinence pads are free on the NHS when assessed as being needed. Some causes of incontinence cannot be cured, but at least they can be socially contained so that you're not wet and smelling of pee. It is certainly true that there are some poor care homes where patients' pads are not changed as often as they should be, but remember that the pads are designed to contain the incontinence while leaving the person dry (essentially big nappies), so just because a pad is wet does not mean there is a problem.

Bowels

If you need to go to the loo several times a day due to an upset stomach, painful spasms or cramping, or a bloated feeling, this could well be a sign of irritable bowel syndrome, the most common digestive disorder. IBS is likely to be something you've had all your life and is rarely a new diagnosis in the elderly. The condition may affect people differently, but never in a good way, and it can result in depression and a poorer quality of life. It is another problem affecting both men and women, although the latter are perhaps more sensible about seeking advice.

Conversely, constipation can be quite common as you get older. Don't let it build up to become a major problem over weeks, because it can make you feel awful. Quite a lot of elderly people are admitted to hospital as an emergency purely due to constipation. The key sign is only a change in frequency from your normal as there's no such thing as 'normal frequency' for people in general; some go once a week throughout their whole life, others feel terrible if they don't go three times a day.

Be open and frank with your GP: there's no need to be embarrassed. And don't be concerned about having a colonoscopy, which may be done to exclude colitis and cancer as a cause of symptoms. Yes, it entails having something pushed up your bottom, but for many it can be quick and painless.

Double incontinence may be common but not inevitable in the very old, but not in the general older population. It depends on cause and is probably not curable, but at least it's containable with pads.

Advanced neurological conditions like MS can cause double incontinence, as can strokes, but usually because sufferers can't get to the toilet, not that actual control has gone. This is 'functional incontinence' – there is nothing wrong with the person's ability to know that they need to go, but as they can't get themselves to a toilet or cope with their underclothes they can end up incontinent. Probably the commonest cause of double incontinence is advanced dementia – there's nothing wrong with the person's bladder or bowels but they have lost social control of them (like babies before potty training).

I have found no specific advice for sufferers of flatulence other than that they should ensure that their hearing aids are working when in public.

Bones and muscles

It's impossible to put a figure on how many of us suffer from aches and pains as we age, but some degree of degenerative arthritis is pretty much inevitable as you grow older. Almost everyone suffers to some degree some of the time.

Keeping fit to whatever level you can manage will certainly help maintain muscle strength, which in turn supports the joints affected by arthritis. Keeping weight under control is also good – lots of fat people puff into arthritis clinics complaining of pain in their knees, but this is hardly surprising when they are putting several stones of extra weight on their joints.

Osteoporosis is 'brittle bones' and almost inevitable to some degree in post-menopausal women, although it also occurs in men. Contrary to popular belief, osteoporosis does not cause bone

Be open and frank with your GP: there's no need to be embarrassed. And don't be concerned about having a colonoscopy.

Spending hours slumped in front of a TV or at your PC on a poor chair is unwise, especially if you are often leaning forward to peer at the screen.

....

pain; indeed you probably won't know you've got it until you break a bone. Your doctor may suggest a bone scan. Note that it is a low trauma that suggests osteoporosis – such as breaking your hip when slipping on a carpeted floor, perhaps; a broken bone if you are hit by a car can happen at any age!

Backache

This is the UK's leading cause of disability, with over a million sufferers and with the majority of the population affected in some way at some time. Causes are mostly muscular and posture related. As we age, too, some degenerative arthritis in the spine is also common.

Spending hours slumped in front of a TV or at your PC on a poor chair is unwise, especially if you are often leaning forward to peer at the screen. Sit upright, although not too rigidly. You may find that yoga or Pilates will help.

The fashion for 'man bags' is causing many men back problems, partly because of the weight of electronic gizmos carried inside them; it is not reported whether man boobs cause the same problem…

Arthritis

This is caused when cartilage between the bones breaks down so that the bones grind together. Symptoms include aches and pains in the joints, or swollen joints with no apparent explanation.

Your doctor should be able to diagnose the condition following a physical examination and possibly more elaborate tests. In older people an X-ray is common. Most arthritis in elderly people is osteoarthritis, essentially wear and tear. A strenuous job or a previous injury can make arthritis in that region more likely. Or it could simply be due to Sod's Law. It won't help to be overweight.

Don't rush off to live in hot climes if you are diagnosed with arthritis. What you feel is a marked improvement may simply be because the change of environment has given you a psychological boost, with no guarantee that it will last.

Treatment will be mostly by painkillers, starting with paracetamol and working up the analgesic ladder as far as morphine, if necessary. Anti-inflammatory painkillers can be helpful too, but older people should be careful about using them regularly for longer than a few weeks because of potential side-effects; take special care if self-medicating with over-the-counter products. Physiotherapy may also help, but there are often waiting lists on the NHS. Chiropractors/ osteopaths might help as well, but choose a reputable one. Other exercise therapies may help too.

Really severe cases of arthritis may need hip and knee replacements; other joints are replaced much less frequently.

The vast majority of (newly diagnosed) arthritis in older people is just wear and tear, but your GP may refer you to a rheumatologist if it is particularly severe or doesn't settle with simple treatment.

Gout

This can occur in both sexes and technically at any age, although it is commoner as we get older. It is true that over-consumption of port can trigger an attack, but it sometimes strikes out of the blue. It is not particularly common.

Limbs

You will improve your chances of not hitting trouble and breaking limbs if you avoid clutter in your home that you could trip over – and have handrails fitted and good lighting where necessary.

Hips

A broken hip needs urgent attention. The target for treatment is within 24 hours, because this is shown to have a better outcome: people get back on their feet more quickly and are less likely to die. The death rate is so high after a fractured hip because breaking the hip in the first place is a marker of general frailty in some people. They don't die as a direct consequence of the fracture, but it can mark the 'beginning of the end'.

Knees

The knee is a mechanically more complex joint than the hip, so hip replacements became common a lot more quickly than new knees. As technicians and doctors perfected the metalwork and the techniques, though, knee ops became more routine and relatively straightforward. I've heard of a 99-year-old who did very well after bilateral total knee replacements.

Feet

I saw a sign in a podiatrist's office reading 'Time wounds all heels'. Don't assume that it will happen to you, but problems with the feet can be painful so pay attention to them. And check between the toes – a fertile area for infections.

Choose footwear more for comfort than fashion – you will be less likely to have a fall if comfortably shod. And don't forget comfortable socks. There is no point in buying shoes to give your feet space if you then clad them in socks or tights that are constricting. Don't have socks tight round the legs, either, because this reduces circulation.

Hello George, what's new?

Both hips and a knee

ROGER LATHAM

Don't let nails grow long and clawlike. If you can't keep them in good order yourself, find a chiropodist. Many will make home visits.

Hard skin? There has been a craze recently (a crazy craze, in my book) for fish pedicures in which small, toothless carp eat away dead skin. But the health authorities are looking into such treatments, which anyway must appal all right-thinking anglers as well as fish and chip lovers everywhere. Those who have had a fish pedicure report that it tickles like hell for the first minute or two but is then not unpleasant. Still sounds fishy to me.

Skin

Skin demonstrates the effects of ageing more obviously than any other part of us. We tend to think of skin as just something to wrap the rest of us in, but it is in fact our largest organ. Air conditioning in the workplace may dry anyone's skin and be a contributory factor in ageing, while skin becomes drier as we get older which may mean it itches – and that may mean we scratch so we could get sores. Old-age eczema occurs as a result of the skin drying – fewer 'fat pockets' and less water-holding properties result in dry skin and itching. Stop using soap and moisturise a lot.

- The cancer risks of excess tanning are, or should be, well known, but tanning may also help produce the leathery 'crocodile skin' look just as smoking does.

- For older people, the risks from the sun are not just to the skin – hot weather can be a problem for those with heart problems or suffering from breathing difficulties.

- The old bruise more easily than the young and this tendency may be heightened by medication such as aspirin and warfarin that thin the blood. The bruises go away in time but can look unsightly.

- Age spots are sun induced; they are not serious but treatments are available if they bother you cosmetically.

- The red noses (rosacea) sported by Rudolph and some men are not provenly due to whisky consumption, although it is likely to contribute. Rosacea can make the nose red and bulky; it can be treated by laser/IPL plus a decrease in alcohol.

For older people, the risks from the sun are not just to the skin – hot weather can be a problem for those with heart problems or suffering from breathing difficulties.

- For leg veins, sclerosing solutions work well. The thread veins are injected with an irritant which causes a small clot that the body clears over a few weeks. For varicose veins, which are more prominent, see a vascular surgeon and consider wearing proper compression hosiery which supports the veins. While this is fine in winter, it can be too hot in summer.

- If you are regretting those tattoos you had done years ago removal is not painful, although the results are variable. Amateur tattoos, consisting only of black ink and therefore more superficial, often clear better than professional tattoos where ink went deeper and colours were used. If, conversely, you are a real granny swinger, I am not aware of any risk in having tattoos done when old.

- To keep your skin looking good:

  - Avoid soap (which is drying) – use soap substitutes.
  - There's no need for toners, which dry the skin. (Male readers may need to consult their partner over this section.)
  - Use lots of moisturising creams (cheap and cheerful ones) – quantity is more important than quality.
  - Having repeatedly advised against salt, one time you need a large pinch of it is when reading cosmetic ads.

- If you are out in the sun, use plenty of cream (generally people don't use enough) and remember the unexpected areas – people have had holidays ruined by forgetting to protect the tops of their feet, for instance. Be most cautious between 11am and 3pm (the boozy siesta time has its advantages) and keep in mind that the weather being overcast does not mean you can't burn.

- Few people bother, but sun blocking daily in the UK between early April and the end of August makes sense.

- If you have many flat brown/black moles, 'mole mapping' (where a picture is taken and then comparisons made on subsequent visits) may be worthwhile, as it is more likely to pick up pre-cancerous skin changes. You then need an expert consultant dermatologist to look at the skin.

Plastic surgery and other cosmetic treatments

- Liposuction to remove fat is an invasive surgery. It is not risk free and it is not a magical cure-all. It tends to work best on stubborn areas of younger, well-toned skin and is probably not an option for an older body shape.

- When an old person, or someone who looks like your mother or father, looks back at you in the mirror, some people rush to have a face lift. The usual advice applies about choosing your surgeon carefully.

- Less expensive and more readily available are treatments given in high-street clinics such as botulinum toxin (commonly referred to as Botox, although this is actually the trade name of one brand of the product) and filler injections. Put simply, Botox paralyses the muscles so that the skin can't crease any more, while fillers plump up the fold when the crease has become permanent. Done well they can really freshen your appearance. Expect people to notice that you look really well and rested, not to look like you did 20 years ago. But remember that it will not cure basic unhappiness if that's what drove you to have the treatment in the first place.

- Study some of the frozen looks and trout-pouts of 'C' list celebrities for examples of bad cosmetic work before you rush into anything. The gossip magazines are full of lurid stories of when things went badly wrong. But if you feel it's for you, choose your cosmetic practitioner very, very carefully. Currently this field is not as regulated as one might wish and people can put up a sign advertising treatments after just doing a brief course.

- Laser treatment? It needs careful evaluation and individual assessment.

- Breast enhancement? After the major scandal recently? Again, it's up to you, but it's perhaps not really something to have in older age and an individual assessment is obviously needed. Might it not be better to buy a more flattering bra or find a short-sighted boyfriend?

- Whatever treatment you are considering:

  – To stress the earlier point: check service providers very carefully. It's a growth area and there are conmen and conwomen around as well as a black market in cosmetic products. It's another area where the internet needs treating with considerable care.
  – Even greater caution is needed if going abroad for treatment, either to save money or to combine with a holiday. You may be offered treatment which would not be allowed in the UK and, in addition, you may find insurance cover impossible while legal redress may not be easy if something goes wrong.
  – The cheapest option is to be realistic. Be happy in your own skin and remember that most of the glamour photographs you see have featured extensive airbrushing. Real life is not like that.

Hair

- Nobody seems really sure why we go grey, as most people do with age, but the process stems from the loss/reduction of melanin – a pigment which gives hair its colour – from hair follicles. The more pigment you lose, the greyer and whiter your hair becomes.

- It is possible to develop an allergy from dyeing your hair and you may get damaged hair shafts from the chemicals, resulting in brittle, dry hair.

- Some 60% of women may be affected by hair loss by the time they are 50. This may be due to heredity but there could be other causes, such as the menopause. The condition may need full medical assessment, and whether hair loss treatments work may depend on the condition. Magic 'hair re-growth pills' are somewhat unproven.

- If it is any consolation for men, baldness is often linked to virility. Hippocrates, who was apparently quite a wise old guy, pointed out in around 400BC that only eunuchs suffered no hair loss.

- Hair loss solutions include:
  – Hair transplants, although watch for scars from pinch grafts which may show as the hair recedes further (as it probably will).
  – As Shakespeare so nearly put it: 'Toupee or not toupee, that is the question.' But take care with wigs or you may look as if you have a catnapping cat on your cranium.
  – Comb-overs invariably look ludicrous, which is why I favour one because of the endless amusement it gives my relatives and friends.

- While the concentration may be on the hair on top of the head, for men a beard may cover a multitude of chins but might also look as if the head is on upside down. Hair in the ears and in particular the nostrils is unappealing and should be removed. You may, of course, wish to defoliate elsewhere, but I feel that is beyond the scope of this book.

Eyes

- You should have your eyes tested every two years until you are 70, and every year thereafter; tests are free for the over 60s (the Scots get them free at any age). Home tests should also be free if you are over 60 and not able to visit the optician.

It is possible to develop an allergy from dyeing your hair and you may get damaged hair shafts from the chemicals, resulting in brittle, dry hair.

You should have regular eye tests because:

- Poor vision can lead to falls
- Poor vision could make you unfit to drive. If you have certain conditions like cataracts and glaucoma you must inform the DVLA and fill in a medical questionnaire. Go to www.direct.gov.uk/motoring to download the form. Be honest, otherwise your car insurance could be invalid.
- Increasingly, you need good eyesight to read the clauses some suppliers slip into their small print.

● When you buy new glasses, keep in mind:

- Stylish and fashionable frames with famous names plastered over them won't actually make you see any better. It's the lenses that do that.
- If going into a care home, have your name marked on the glasses to avoid any mix-ups. This will be cheaper than changing your name to Pierre Cardin.
- Contact lenses may not work for everyone.

- Ready-made glasses from shops should only be used as a short-term solution, perhaps for reading if you have broken or lost your glasses. It's probably better to keep your last set of glasses to hand for such emergencies.
- With any new spectacles, and bi- or tri-focals in particular, take care for a few days while becoming familiar with them, especially when going down stairs. Not everyone can get used to them and some people take weeks to do so.

● You can, of course, consider laser treatment so that you don't need to wear glasses at all, but by no means everyone is suitable. If you take this route, check the qualifications and success rate of whoever is performing the operation, and do read all the promotional material carefully. It's one of just many areas where word of mouth is the best way of finding someone. A good, respectable clinic will turn a lot of people down because the risks are too high in certain cases. Remember, laser correction of your lifelong

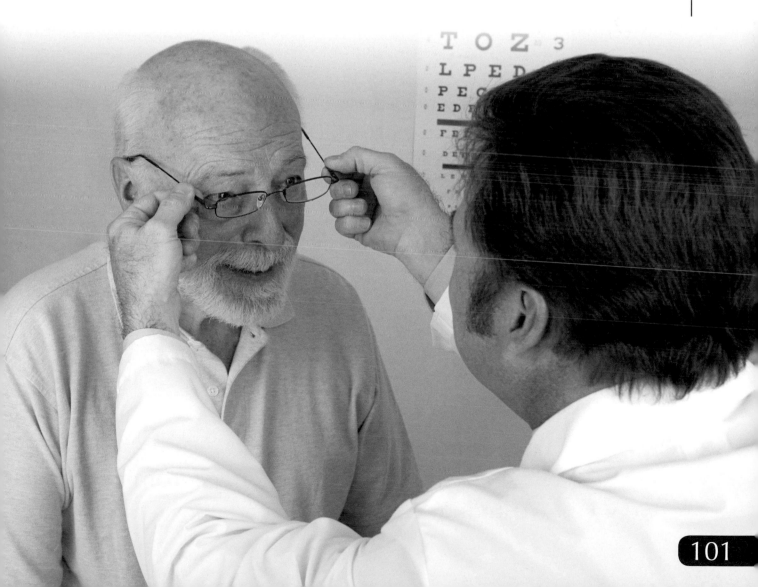

short-sightedness won't stop the eventual 'arms too short' need for reading glasses as you get older; that is virtually inevitable to some degree.

- But, and an important but, having your eyes tested is not just a case of reading off a chart, then ordering new glasses. A test has another important role: it may reveal other conditions that need treating.

- Cataracts reduce the amount of light passing through the lenses in your eyes. They cause your vision to become cloudy or opaque. Cataracts can be treated by surgery, during which an artificial lens is inserted. This is now a routine procedure and can be done on quite frail people very successfully. No general anaesthetic is necessary; it's all done under a local.

- Glaucoma can cause blindness. There are two main types. One causes sudden painful loss of vision and needs urgent treatment. The type picked up by opticians, on the other hand, is diagnosed by checking your intra-ocular pressures by blowing a puff of air into the eye. This test by the optician is not definitive, but if your pressure is a bit raised they will refer you to an eye clinic for more sophisticated tests. The treatment is eye drops. (It is believed that only half of sufferers know that they have glaucoma.)

- Age-related macular degeneration (AMD) affects the light-sensitive lining of the eye, the retina. The central part of this lining is the macula and governs what we see straight in front of us. AMD is most common in the over 55s, and smoking heavily increases the risk of developing it. New drugs and other treatments are now available that work for some.

- Opticians are sometimes the people who diagnose diabetes, when they see the retinal changes of diabetic eye disease. Similarly, long-standing badly controlled high blood pressure can cause retinal changes. Both are important to pick up as they can be treated but can cause blindness if left untreated.

- All these and other eye problems can be treated, but the earlier such conditions are identified the better. If you notice a sudden change in your eyes, get them checked; don't wait until the one or two years are up before your next test is due.

   If I can inject a personal note here, a routine eye test suggested my cataracts might need attention so I saw an ophthalmologist. The cataracts didn't need work … but a detached retina did. As a devout coward I was scared stiff, as I suspect many others would be at the thought of any eye operation. In fact it was quick and painless and changed my view of such work. So don't be squeamish. Have your eyes checked.

If you notice a sudden change in your eyes, get them checked; don't wait until the one or two years are up before your next test is due.

How often should people have a dental check? Well, a good, clean, healthy mouth probably need only be checked every 12 to 18 months.

Teeth

Teeth came last on my survey of friends' health concerns, but they are still an important area because gum disease and decay are the most prevalent conditions in the world today, beating cancer and heart disease.

There are now new fields of dentistry specifically for the elderly, and these include implants. People are living and retaining their teeth for far longer than previously, and new techniques have been developed to cope with the wear associated with this longevity. Implants are now used to replace missing teeth – and if no teeth are present the dentures can be bolted to the jaw bones.

The oral care from either nursing homes or home helps may not always be as good as it should be. Thank goodness, though, that the older we get the more resistant our teeth seem to be to the presence of food around them.

The main concern for many elderly people is the problem of 'dry mouth syndrome' which is caused by age or medication and can lead to rampant decay and problems with dentures. It can be treated with artificial saliva or simply regular rinsing with water.

The golden rule with teeth is to keep them clean, especially the spaces in between where most problems start. This is achieved with either dental floss or small interdental brushes. Brush after breakfast and last thing at night. Always brush away from the gums, never up and down or sideways. If a dry mouth exists, a fluoride mouthwash will help to reduce decay.

Electric toothbrushes are great, but they have to be used properly or they will do more damage than a conventional toothbrush. They can reach the parts that other brushes cannot and have larger handles which benefit arthritic patients.

How often should people have a dental check? Well, a good, clean, healthy mouth probably need only be checked every 12 to 18 months. What is important is what the person does every day at home, not what the dentist does in the surgery every six months or so. It is a sliding scale dependent upon factors such as smoking, standard of oral hygiene, the presence of fillings, gum disease, etc.

NHS treatment is free to those under 18, and for anyone who is pregnant or has a child under one year old (because pregnancy and its immediate aftermath are known to increase the risk of tooth decay in the mother). It's also free to those on certain benefits – check if this applies in your case. There are three bands of treatment – simple, not so simple, and complex, with the patient paying part.

As we age our teeth become darker naturally. The outer covering of teeth, the enamel, wears thin over the years and allows the dentine layer underneath, which is a much darker colour, to show through more. It is an irony that the more we brush our teeth over the years, to keep them clean and white, the more we are wearing away the enamel and making them darker! Always brush gently. You do not scrub any other part of your body with a brush twice a day (or at least I hope you don't, because it would hurt). Whitening treatments are available but, as always, take care to use reputable operators.

If 'going private' for any dental treatment, agree costs in advance. You might care to insure against dental costs. With a dental insurance scheme you then pay the bill and claim from the insurance company. With a dental maintenance scheme a dentist will get your teeth into good condition and then set a monthly premium. There are various levels of cover; generally, you get what you pay for. But always read the small print.

If you have a good, healthy mouth, don't get involved in contact sports and only need an annual visit to the dentist, then it is better to pay as you go. If you need more regular visits, or might need treatment at some stage and want to budget for that treatment, then a dental maintenance scheme should suit you. Patients on such schemes tend to turn up regularly for a check-up as they have paid for it. The dentist is not paid extra for any treatment needed, so it is in his interest to keep your mouth in good condition.

Finally, if you go into hospital or move to a care home, it helps to have your name on your false teeth, to avoid mix-ups. A dentist friend had to visit a lady in a home to make new dentures. It seemed the lady in the next bed had died during the night and, in the rush and the dark, the staff had put the wrong dentures into the deceased. 'They've gone and burned my good teeth!' she told him.

MOBILITY

Movement can be a great confidence booster and can avoid people feeling 'trapped' and helpless. If mobility starts to become a problem, see a doctor. The longer you bravely soldier on, putting up with something, the harder it may be to recover. Your difficulty may well be treatable or, at least, have a solution.

Fortunately for those with mobility problems, there is a huge range of equipment available to help. If you can only blink an eye or move a little finger then technology may enable you to communicate and do things, whether to increase mobility or handle incontinence. However, it is important to get yourself properly diagnosed and assessed before acquiring anything. Your condition might even become worse with the wrong equipment.

You will be given the essential equipment you need by health and social services, albeit not in a choice of colours and styles, so there is no need to buy anything essential. You may choose to buy other things you want, like riser-recliner chairs, but a word of warning: there may be rip-off merchants selling unsuitable or overpriced equipment so if possible consult other users of the item you are thinking of purchasing. You must try before you buy.

Most areas have suppliers with wide ranges of equipment on display, and a local service may be the most convenient and helpful. If possible, also visit one of the major shows, like Naidex, where you will find a great display of products, as well as seminars covering various disability issues.

The help available is not just mechanical. There is, for instance, clothing for the disabled – jeans with large zips for people with restricted use of their hands; longer zips for easier access to catheterise; no projections at the back of clothing so no pressure problems if a wheelchair user – and so on. In this chapter I'll be looking at a small selection of aids.

Walking sticks

- These will help keep your muscles working better than sitting in a wheelchair, and they are available with a choice of handle grips.

- Get professionally assessed by a therapist who will know how to adjust a stick to the right height for you. (At various points you may come across both physiotherapists and occupational therapists – both need degree courses and they are highly trained and well able to assess what's right for you.)

- Have a loop for the wrist so that you don't drop the stick; simple brackets are available to hang a stick on a dining table.

- The rubber bung on the bottom (the ferule) is the equivalent of the tyres on a car: if the tread is bald it won't grip and you may slip and fall. Don't teeter around with a handsome antique cane with a wooden tip.

- It is perhaps easy to mock those using walking poles when just going to the shops, but they do help you to keep your balance and can take a lot of strain off your knees, particularly when going downhill.

Walkers

- Zimmer frames are absolutely the right thing for a lot of people, but you must, must, must be assessed first. Frames alter your gait pattern quite significantly, which may make walking strength worse with the wrong choice.

- Walkers with two wheels and two legs are fine for limited areas and for people lacking confidence – say after an operation.

- Three-wheeled ones are compact and very manoeuvrable – they will turn within themselves – and are perhaps the best indoor type and useful in restricted areas like shops. You need a handbrake when turning yourself around. They will fold flat for carrying in cars.

- Those with four wheels, often with a built-in shelf and seat, are the most stable but take up more space. They will fold, although maybe not completely flat. Again, a handbrake is essential.

- For those assessed as needing a frame, the information regarding ferules is the same as for walking sticks.

Walkers with two wheels and two legs are fine for limited areas and for people lacking confidence – say after an operation.

- Various bags have been designed to attach to the frame, so that you can carry stuff from room to room – therapists will usually assess for these too. Those needing a frame for all mobility will often need a trolley, too, so that they can still walk while carrying a plate of food or a drink.

- It is not unknown for a walker to be used as a rail on which to dry smalls in front of a fire.

Scooters & wheelchairs

- The advice to 'use it or lose it' and keep as active as possible is sound, but stubbornly carrying on when it's patently too much for you, so that you're utterly jiggered all the time, is not a good thing. There may come a time when a scooter or wheelchair would help.

- As with other equipment, get assessed! You can refer yourself, or be referred by a GP, to a wheelchair clinic which will assess you for an NHS chair to meet your needs. A possible exception to the need for assessment would be a carer-propelled chair for going round shops, where the person can walk, but just not that far. Self-propelled chairs are a completely different matter and should only be used after assessment – few frail older people have the upper body strength to use them anyway.

- Electric wheelchairs (operated by a joystick on the armrest, as opposed to scooters which have handlebars more like a motorbike) should only be bought after proper assessment that they are suitable for you. You may not have to pay for an electric wheelchair if the therapist thinks your need is great enough.

Right: The author is by no means alone in considering Sir Stirling Moss the greatest racing driver of all time. Here he demonstrates an important part of using scooters and wheelchairs – properly adjusted mirrors.

- Consult other wheelchair users, then draw up your own 'wants' list before buying. There is no point in buying one guaranteed to climb every mountain if you are afraid of heights.

- Think about what weather protection you may need. A full-weather framed transparent cover is available but may perhaps be a bit of overkill; a good showerproof jacket, a hat and a plastic sheet or apron to cover the legs is usually sufficient. The sheet can be used to cover the seat when parked.

- Use the biggest amp/hour battery you can fit. It is advisable to specify a jelly electrolyte as distinct from a liquid acid one as they stand up to rough surfaces better. Indicators on the instrument panels of bigger scooters will show the state of the battery.

- Practise in a quiet area before more venturesome travel, and seek expert advice when learning, not least because some electric vehicles really do have quite fearsome acceleration. Care is especially needed at pedestrian crossings when waiting at a light. Keep your hand well away from the speed control (there have been cases of accidents where this has been pressed accidentally, with alarming results). Sensitive control is possible if the speed range knob is turned to low and a gentle hand is used on the speed range lever. (Road-legal scooters have a knob which selects a speed range of 0–4mph for pavements and 0–10mph for roads.)

- In general, scooters are well constructed and stand a lot of punishment. A major worry can be punctures, though, as many are fitted with the tubed type of tyre. A puncture is no fun for anyone, least of all a disabled scooter driver. However, puncture-proof tyres are available and although they produce a harder ride they give the rider much more confidence.

Other points to remember

- Check service and maintenance back-up.
- Try the weight. And check the ease of collapsing, e.g. to stow away or put in a car boot.
- If available, all items are cheaper second-hand and most have had little wear, for obvious reasons. Websites are worth a trawl, as are classified ads in local papers.
- If possible, take someone with a little mechanical knowledge with you when viewing.
- Remember you can lease vehicles under the excellent Motability scheme, while many towns offer Shopmobility schemes where, by joining, usually for a nominal donation, you will be given a membership number and a brief familiarisation with the scooter or wheelchair you wish to use on

future shopping visits. You can usually park in a disabled space with Shopmobility.
- Check that no medicines you take could affect your driving. In other words, be just as sensible as if driving a car.
- Don't drink and drive. There is no law against it (didn't someone once say the law was an ass?) but it clearly isn't sensible.
- Watch your speed if surface conditions are wet or icy. If you do have to go out in poor weather wear warm clothing and advise someone of your travel plans.
- Third party insurance is strongly recommended because of the possibility of damage to shop equipment, doors, windows and pedestrians' ankles. Legal and damage claims, as well as insurance against theft, can often be incorporated into your house insurance.
- You may need a ramp to load your machine into a car. Most public service vehicles offer help or have vehicles equipped for loading.
- Do keep an eye on the range. That for pavement scooters can be short, especially if there are gradients on your route.
- Take care on sloping ground – the brakes are not friction type so are not progressive. They lock the wheels and are really only for parking.
- Road-legal scooters with three or four wheels are bigger and more bulky, but have a much better driving position because of having more space. They also have road-legal lights, signals and a horn.

Cars

- If you need a car when disabled, it is worth visiting either a local or national show (such as the Mobility Show at Peterborough) where you can see and try a wide range of vehicles equipped with mobility aids. Check whether the doors open wide enough and the sills are easy to negotiate, and consider what extras you may need to address your particular problem. But don't get carried away. Take a simple thing, like a swivel seat to help you get into a car. There are many available, but a plastic supermarket bag laid on the seat may help your bottom to swivel just as well.

Watch your speed if surface conditions are wet or icy. If you do have to go out in poor weather wear warm clothing and advise someone of your travel plans.

- Keep in mind, by the way, that the Motability scheme under which you lease a car, typically for three years, does not cover speeding fines.

- If you are disabled you may be entitled to a Blue Badge, which also applies to those chauffeuring a disabled person, provided that person is in the car at the time. The badges are being redesigned to make them more difficult to forge by able-bodied oafs – a clampdown on offenders seems likely: quite right too. On a more positive note, many products are available for Blue Badge users such as mobile phone apps and satnavs that will direct you to disabled parking bays.

- As important as the Blue Badge can be a Radar Key, which gives access to several thousand disabled toilets throughout the UK.

- As the number of disabled drivers grows, it is likely that we will see more independent mobility assessments units; a doctor with whom you have a cosy relationship may not be the most impartial person to judge if you qualify for a precious Blue Badge.

When to stop driving

If you are over 70 the DVLA needs you to confirm that you have no medical condition that could affect your ability to drive, and thereafter your licence has to be renewed every three years. There should be no problem, provided you can satisfactorily answer the medical questions on later application forms

If you have certain conditions, such as heart problems and poor vision, then the law says you should notify the DVLA. Not everyone does this, which is stupid, because apart from the obvious danger to other people from such conditions, combined with slower reactions by older drivers, non-notification could well be seized upon by insurers to challenge a claim.

The DVLA issues detailed guidelines for doctors, and it's their job to tell you when you have a condition that should be notified. If you refuse to stop driving voluntarily and pose a risk to other road users because of your condition the doctor has a legal duty to shop you to the DVLA (so is allowed to waive confidentiality).

But, I hear you cry, 'Older drivers don't

travel so many miles.' No – but statistics suggest that the over 80s have more accidents per mile than any other age bracket.

How can you get someone to stop driving?

- Suggest visiting a place offering simulation tests, to give an objective assessment of reaction times and so forth.

- Convey the concern of their nearest and dearest and hope they will respect those feelings, putting out of their head any idea that relatives are either worried about funeral expenses or covet their car.

- Perhaps point out that there are advantages in scootering (although people can still be dangerous on them) such as the ease of getting to local sporting activities, the local park, even the local pub without the hassle of traffic or parking.

- Repeatedly pressing a non-existent foot brake when you are their passenger may send out the right signal, as may whimpering and clutching the dashboard.

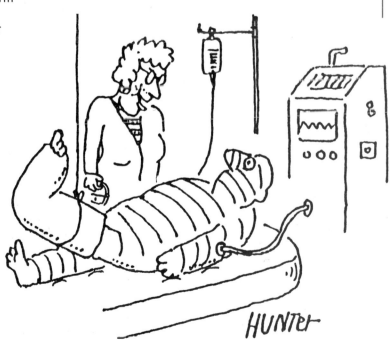

*'You should have known I meant
"left" when I said "right".'*

HOME AIDS

Don't be too proud to use aids if they can help you with a problem. Search online or via Yellow Pages or in libraries for local centres where you can view what is available and take impartial advice; some may have complete rooms fitted with all the relevant aids.

You may be surprised by the range of equipment available, but don't splash out on anything without proper assessment and advice. Therapists may be available at some centres for private consultation.

As with the mobility items mentioned in the previous chapter, local health authorities are likely to provide a complete service with regard to installing handrails, including those to assist getting in and out of a bed, bath or shower, fitting equipment to raise chairs, special toilet seats and so on. While some adaptations may be means tested, all basic required equipment is provided free and although the system won't generally provide other things, it would advise on the appropriateness (or not) of something you were thinking of buying.

Emergency call systems

With these call systems, if you press an alarm button worn either round your neck, on your wrist or clipped to your clothing, then the phone will ring in a control centre. The staff there will try to identify what help you need. They may call, in turn, a list of friends and relatives whom you have nominated as points of contact, until they find someone able to come to you as soon as possible. If there is no reply from anyone they will call the emergency services.

Most alarm equipment can be either bought or rented, and fitting will be done by the supplier. A simpler and cheaper variation – although slightly larger to carry around all the time – would be a mobile phone with a panic button, which causes three or four numbers to be called when pressed.

Handrails

- Many disabled people move by what is known as 'handing', that is, moving from one piece of furniture to another, thus achieving unbroken support. Such an approach is not without risk, however. If people are that unsteady they need to be assessed for an appropriate walking aid such as a Zimmer frame.

- People with balance problems or unsteady legs should resist boldly moving anywhere without something to hang on to, whether furniture or handrails. This particularly applies in kitchens where they may be carrying plates or cutlery – that's what trolleys are for. It is not a good idea to buy more and more equipment to compensate for a disability without having that disability properly diagnosed and assessed – in some cases it might even be reversible with the right treatment.

- A handrail should always be fitted where there are steps.

Bathing aids

There are bath hoists available that are helpful for either self- or assisted bathing, and there are also walk-in baths. While some people like these, many dispense with baths altogether and go for a wet room with no steps. A carer can shower you in a wet room (possibly getting quite wet in the process) if you can't manage on your own, but they can't properly assist you in a bath of any sort.

Remember that a bathroom can be a danger area, with a slippery floor and the risk of falling.

Stairlifts and ramps

- Don't have a stairlift installed just because you are too lazy to walk upstairs. Stairs, taken slowly, with adequate handrails, can be useful exercise to keep muscles strong.

- The wait for a stairlift from social services can be very long in some areas.

If you are thinking of having a ramp built – for easier access to your home, for instance – seek professional advice and assessment first.

If you are thinking of having a ramp built – for easier access to your home, for instance – seek professional advice and assessment first.

- If you are paying for your own stairlift they are often advertised, on eBay and in classified ads, but few people are capable of fitting them properly. Some can be hired, which may be a better option if a disability is temporary, say for a broken bone, or if a person is only expected to live for a few months.

- It is essential that a stairlift is battery operated with automatic charging so that it functions during a power cut, otherwise you could be stranded at the wrong end of the stairs until the electricity comes back on.

- Advise friends and relatives how the thing works.

- Keep the phone number of the service company to hand.

- If you are thinking of having a ramp built – for easier access to your home, for instance – seek professional advice and assessment first.

Ease & safety in the home

- Encourage visitors to put things back where they found them. There is often a special reason why they were there in the first place.

- If a person has weak arm muscles, blinds which open and close with a slight pull of a cord will be a lot easier than having to draw curtains.

- A net or box to catch mail will stop you having to bend to pick up letters; a trigger-operated stick may be useful for picking up other items from the floor.

'The Double Deluxe gets both of you upstairs before you can forget why you're going.'

Time switches on a light or two when you are out, and outside lights triggered by sensors, may be a deterrent.

- Most electrical sockets are at floor level. Ready made-up extension leads are available so that an outlet can be raised, but for increased safety it may be worth having an electrician move sockets up to counter height.

- Have emergency lighting on hand. A rechargeable or wind-up torch, for instance, should always be near your bed so that there is no need to go searching in the dark.

Home security

Security measures make sense whether or not you are disabled or in retirement, and are worth outlining here.

- Only you can judge whether Neighbourhood Watch schemes are a significant deterrent. When, as an experiment, police officers in plain clothes prowled round an estate in Oxford over several evenings, trying car doors and windows, peering over fences and rattling window catches, not one resident dialled 999!

- Expensive-looking houses may not be the most at risk as burglars may suspect the owners can afford good alarm systems and locks.

- Time switches on a light or two when you are out, and outside lights triggered by sensors, may be a deterrent.

- If you move to a fresh property, consider changing all the locks.

- Destroy old keys. Most households will have hoards of them.

- Never leave keys on show.

- Have important emergency phone numbers to hand.

- If you're having building work done, consider having a safe built in somewhere. One of those 'safes' made of dummy books or baked bean tins will be better than nothing for small items, but perhaps change the labels on any you buy because burglars visit shops and craft fairs too.

Smoke alarms

It's easy to forget about these, or forget to maintain them, but talk to firemen and they will tell you how misguided this approach can be.

Safety chains and bars

- Small cost, big peace of mind; consider a spyhole too.

- Don't keep a guard on all the time, only when you have unknown callers. You may need to leave in an emergency, or a carer with a key may not be able to get in.

- Chains or bars (the latter may be easier to use) need to be strong enough to withstand a firm kick.

Bogus callers

- Crooks are becoming more and more plausible. They are quite likely to be smartly dressed and carrying what appears to be correct identification. If in doubt, phone the council or the company they claim to represent; genuine callers will not resent this. But look the number up in a directory – don't take it off their ID card as that may simply put you through to an accomplice.

- Because of the concerns raised, some utility companies and other organisations offer safeguards like password systems. It is worth consulting them about this.

- If someone knocks and says your roof is falling in or they just happen to have enough tarmac left over from another job to do your drive, say 'No'!

- Perhaps have a personal alarm to hand and call police and alert neighbours if you suspect you have had a bogus caller. A description of the person and any vehicle you've spotted will be helpful.

- Callers wishing to convert you to their religious views? Your decision.

Intruders

In our sensitive society, you need be aware of what you can and can't do in repelling intruders. Well, you can use reasonable force to protect yourself and in the heat of the moment you are not expected to make a fine judgement over the level of that force. If you only do what you honestly and instinctively believe is necessary, it would be strong evidence that you acted lawfully and in self-defence. That applies even if you use something as a weapon.

Broadly, the more extreme the circumstances and the more fear you feel, the more force you can lawfully use in self-defence. And if you are genuinely in fear for yourself or others, the law does not require you to wait to be attacked before using defensive force yourself.

Although there are several cases on record where intruders have died after a tussle, the householders were still found to have acted lawfully. But remember that word 'reasonable'. It would not be regarded as reasonable if, suspecting a likely visit from an intruder, you wired all the metal window catches to the mains electricity.

Of course, threats or nuisances may not arrive in person but by post, phone or via the internet. Even if you have signed up for all the available call and mail blocking systems and have installed the best computer security, stuff may still get through.

Asking callers to speak up may put them off, or keep a whistle to hand and blow it down the phone. Vigorously. Alternatively, just hang up or quietly place the receiver by the phone and let them carry on – they are paying for the call, after all.

Nuisance mail or online scams, perhaps telling you that you have won thousands and only need to send £20 or so for administration in order to collect the riches? These are obvious scams, of course, but older people sadly still fall for them. Just remember that if something sounds too good to be true, it is.

If someone knocks and says your roof is falling in or they just happen to have enough tarmac left over from another job to do your drive, say 'No'!

CARE AND CARERS

In your own home

Many people will wish to stay in their own home for as long as possible, even if it means downsizing in order to do so. Indeed, an early decision to downsize may prevent a more complex and daunting task later. Be cautious about moving, though, because unless support is in place your condition could, in fact, deteriorate faster than in a more supportive environment.

Local health authorities are generally very helpful in providing care, but advice from a nearby friend or neighbour is often most people's best way of finding help. They may also suggest day centres to go to, which may stimulate people needing care while at the same time giving carer-relatives a break; such visits will usually be arranged by a social worker.

Workers who have been involved in organised care are often prepared to operate independently for a suitable fee (much of the charge for health care is lost in administration), but most people don't have the luxury of this choice because they don't pay the full cost of their home care; social services do, so you will get what you are given. Also, be wary of independently recruiting someone – all professionals are vetted via Criminal Records Bureau (CRB) checks – because some rogues still slip through; con(wo)men can be very plausible.

Carers supplied by the local authority probably won't have time to chat because, typically, they will have an allocation of 15–30 minutes per client and will therefore be under time pressure. This may not be helpful if you are prescribed, say, a gel that needs a bath or shower every day … but sadly there may not be the funding for carers to make that happen. Doctors should consider this when prescribing, but those who don't routinely work with elderly people may not be aware of possible difficulties. Tell the doctor if you can't use what they've given you. If the care for an individual requires a bath in their own home, the bath or shower will have to be adapted to be safe for both client and carer. And gels and creams create their own issues in making an area more slippery.

Private agencies will provide, for a fee of course, all types of home care: feeding, dressing, cleaning, cooking, shopping, tablet administration, bed making and sheet changing, and so on.

A carer from an organised care company may be a different one each time, which can cause problems with explaining one's needs and the location of equipment, clothing, etc. and, not least, in forging a personal relationship.

Meals

Good nutrition is important at any age, but standing at a cooker or sink can become tiring for an older person, so careful shopping may be important to make use of balanced packaged meals that can be frozen, then popped in a microwave.

Contact your GP about local services available, such as Meals on Wheels, which will be part of a needs assessment. Others, including some people who are not disabled but just incompetent cooks or simply too lazy to make their own meals, may choose one of the commercial meal providers who cater for dietary needs and arrange regular deliveries to suit you and even put the food in the freezer for you. Choosing a week's supply of food and then having it delivered takes away a lot of hassle and may reassure friends/relatives that a person is eating properly.

Don't neglect fluids. The elderly often have a misconception that drinking less fluid will save them from frequent toilet visits. The opposite may be true because, as mentioned in the chapter on physical health, a lack of fluids can cause bladder irritation and increase the risk of urinary tract infection and dehydration.

'I hope you're not thinking of living to be 110…'

Various other living options are available, although that may mean moving area if you want workspace or golf or a spa or other facilities.

Retirement housing and sheltered housing

The next stage, if living alone becomes too much for someone, may be to move in with relatives provided everyone is fully on board with the idea. There may still be difficulty in getting all the support you need and such arrangements don't always work. I know of one case where an elderly relative moved back home after a spell abroad with their family. The relationship had broken down because the family took liberties with free babysitting and childcare duties.

Various other living options are available, although that may mean moving area if you want workspace or golf or a spa or other facilities, and you may then need to find a new GP. Builders and developers are responding to the market for people who may want to scale down, but not in standards. They may avoid the 'retirement' word and just talk about housing being for people over such-and-such an age.

Whatever your choice, you may wish to consider:

● Post and newspapers delivered to your own door?
● Security, such as a camera entry system?
● Pendant alarm switches?
● Good sound insulation between properties?
● Guest rooms on site for visitors to use?
● Any on-site staff?
● If offered a choice of a property overlooking a tranquil garden or a busy street most will opt for the garden view, but in fact a bustling street may be more mentally stimulating than just watching squirrels nibbling nuts.

If a person is choosing for themselves these are all things to consider, but if the choice is being made by carers because the patient now lacks capacity, then as a general rule don't uproot dementia sufferers to a sheltered housing complex because the move will be unsettling and likely to make their confusion worse. When they can't be supported at home, it is best for them to go straight for residential care.

Care homes

Historically there have been residential homes and nursing homes – residential homes do not have to have any qualified nursing staff on shift (although many have nurses as managers etc.). Residential homes vary quite a lot in how disabled a resident can be – some can cope with people who are completely immobile and need hoisting, while others need you to be able to walk with assistance.

Nursing homes take people who need 24/7 availability of qualified nurses (though most care is given by unqualified carers) for things like pressure area care in someone who is bed-bound, monitoring diabetes and giving insulin, or helping people on artificial feeding regimens. Most residents are very dependent. While there are good and bad nursing homes, there is less variability in what level of dependency they will accept.

Quite a lot of homes are 'dual registered,' i.e. both residential and nursing homes are in the same building, usually in different wings or floors and run as separate homes. The theory is that if you are in the residential bit and become more dependent, you have your care needs reassessed and they upgrade you to the nursing side, which of course is likely to mean a change of room.

More innovative places are becoming common where you start out in a flat, living fairly independently, and then as you become frailer the care comes to you rather than you moving to have more care.

Specialist dementia care homes – both residential and nursing – exist. Many people with dementia live in ordinary care homes; the specialist dementia care homes are for those with behavioural problems that are difficult to manage in an ordinary home, e.g. wandering, aggressive behaviour, etc.

If your intention is eventually to go into a home, don't leave it too late to view some and gather all the relevant information. Bear in mind, though, that you aren't generally given the option to go into a care home (unless you pay for it yourself) without trying to cope with a care package at home first. This may be tough on those who are lonely and would prefer a care home for the company, but that's how it is unless you can afford to pay.

All care homes have to be registered with the CQC (Care Quality Commission). The type of place will depend on the level of service you need.

Shock/horror stories of poor care may be alarming, and to a large extent residents are 'captive' in that they can't simply pack and move elsewhere very quickly. But don't despair – there are many excellent places around. You just need to select with care. You may be trying to find somewhere in a hurry and therefore be more likely to err, but you don't get weeks to search while a relative is in hospital either – they may have to go for a temporary bed where one is available and then move from there to the place of choice later.

There may be a good case for finding somewhere near where you already live because you are more likely to have friends visiting you. The value of a peer group popping in and playing impromptu board games and the like cannot be overestimated. And you may need to change your GP if you move out of the area. Some but by no means all care homes may have a GP on call. Where there is a routine weekly visit by a GP the home will almost certainly have paid the local surgery for the service. The closest GP practice to a care home will usually be the GP for the majority of the residents but the amount of input varies widely.

Note how places score on any local rating scheme, although there may be more important things than how targets are being met – sometimes by just ticking boxes. Try to get feedback from others who have used places you are considering. Your GP will probably not, in fact definitely should not, recommend a specific care home; if they do, perhaps check who owns it.

Most care homes will be trying to make a profit and this is not an unreasonable aim, although exercise caution if a place seems to be owned by financial adventurers. Stability is important as you age: witness the despairing faces sometimes shown in the media when residents have to be moved because a home has abruptly closed.

A visit is vital. A glossy website or brochure may conceal many things, but a personal look should give you a feeling for how well (or badly) the place is run.

- Take a list of things that are important for you when visiting homes, otherwise it's only later you'll realise you forgot to check a key point.

- A visit without an appointment is preferable, but be considerate and avoid mealtimes and early mornings. A good time would be between 2pm and 4pm because activities should be in full swing (and you may be given afternoon tea).

- First impressions are important, whether you are visiting yourself or a friend or relative is vetting somewhere for you. Is the doorbell answered quickly and with a smile? Or do staff look harassed?

- Does it smell of pee? No home should, and thanks to modern materials chair coverings can have the appearance and feel of cloth but be completely washable. Obviously a smell could be a bit offputting, but don't be lulled into a false sense of security by a glossy, hotel-like appearance either. And the smell of pee might have come from one person who had an accident in the hall just before you got there – in an otherwise excellent home – so keep an open mind.

- Don't be put off if some residents are sitting glazed in front of a TV. This may be inevitable in even the best-run places.

- Does the place look cheerful, with pictures and flowers here and there? More importantly, will it be able to provide the support and facilities you need? Things like the provision of medical care, night coverage, dental care, a chiropodist, hairdresser, laundry facilities, church services, TV, phone and computer access are all worth checking out.

- Bedrooms should preferably be en-suite, perhaps not with baths but certainly adapted showers with suitable handrails and anti-slip surfaces, plus alarm cords for safety.

- Are there lavatories or mainly commodes?

- Is it possible to take a favourite piece of furniture?

- Is there access for wheelchairs everywhere? This should be a given, of course.

Bedrooms should be en-suite, perhaps not with baths but certainly adapted showers with suitable handrails and anti-slip surfaces, plus alarm cords for safety.

Don't be put off if some residents are sitting glazed in front of a TV. This may be inevitable in even the best-run places.

- A quiet lounge area is useful for reading or craftwork, and for receiving visitors away from the bedroom, in additional to a communal TV/ entertainments lounge.

- If you've been unable to kick the habit, you may want to know if smoking is permitted in your own room (though obviously not in any public areas).

- How flexible are mealtimes? Don't expect the impossible, although residents should be offered a choice of menu daily, especially at lunchtime, with the option of a cooked breakfast at weekends, at the very least. Residents may sometimes prepare their own breakfasts, so that they can get up when they wish.

- What is the home's attitude to visitors – can they drop in anytime? Do they have to sign themselves in and out?

- If there is a guest bedroom for visitors to use, consider staying in it for a few days to see if you really like the place.

- Is it pet friendly? You may, of course, prefer the place not to be!

- Are residents free to come and go as they please?

- Are there any planned leisure activities? Some homes have dedicated social activities officers. But are they the sort of activities that you would enjoy? When I trawled half a dozen care homes with a relative, the managers at two of them seemed surprised when she marched straight out the moment they beamed the word 'bingo'.

- Do residents get any fresh air by being taken into the garden? Assuming they want to go, of course … they are not dogs to be exercised. Are there perhaps gentle exercise classes for residents, to maintain mobility?

- A major factor in the smooth running of a home is the members of staff:

  - Ask about staff turnover. Fresh faces can add variety and be something for residents to gossip about, but a constant stream of new people may be upsetting, especially if this affects more intimate tasks like washing and dressing.
  - Ask what training staff have had, and what ongoing training there is.
  - Ratio of staff to residents? If staff are clearly overstretched at times, would there be any support for a volunteers' group?
  - Do staff speak reasonable English? Ideally all residents should be assigned a key worker to allow one-to-one care with better assessment of needs, and also responsibility for liaison with relatives etc. Other senior staff would be in change of more general matters, GP visits, chiropody and so on.

- It is a good idea for relatives to stitch name labels on clothing – adhesive ones tend to become detached with regular laundering. Mark all possessions, including wheelchairs and walking sticks, and personal items like spectacles or radios to avoid mix-ups. Having an inventory of possessions is a normal practice, but remember to keep it updated if items are taken away or replaced. If a resident wears rings or other valuable jewellery, a sensible safeguard might be to take a dated and timed photograph of them wearing it, witnessed by a member of staff.

- Arrangements for handling the finances of residents will vary from one place to another, but the aim should be for every resident to have a 'personal spending' financial account, with the process controlled by the home's administration, capable of producing monthly statements showing deductions (e.g. newspapers, hairdressing, special shopping) and any additions like supplementary payments made by family, pension payments and so on. There is a formal entitlement for residents to have access to their money; leaving a resident without finance can be interpreted as financial abuse.

- If, despite careful selection, you still have problems with a home, you can refer a complaint to the CQC and your local authority, but do try a friendly approach first. It's always better to settle amicably and on site if you can.

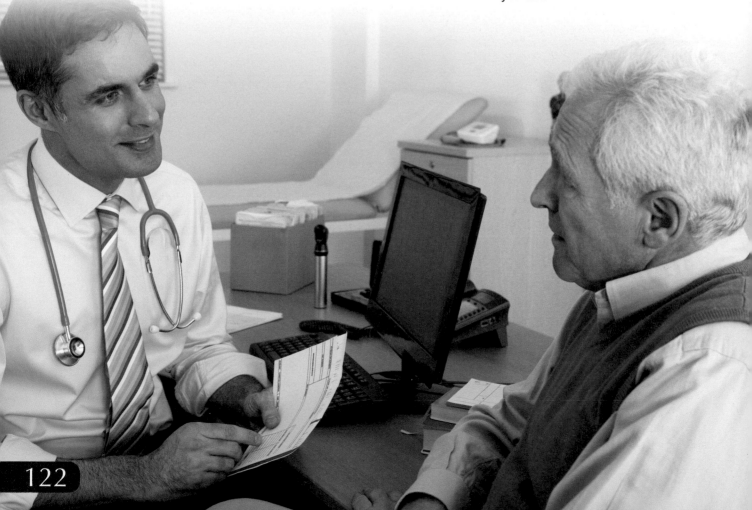

Hospitals

In theory, you have the right to choose which hospital your doctor refers you to, although this is only true of elective outpatient referral. You will have no real choice where you end up if you dial 999. For the most part, this so-called 'choice' tends to be political flannel anyway, because the majority of patients don't want 'choice', they just want to know that their local hospital will do right by them.

Pretty much everywhere will have some sort of intermediate care service. As a general rule, people shouldn't go into a nursing home as a new placement straight from hospital – they should have a more extended period of rehabilitation/recovery in an intermediate care bed before a final decision is made. There will be some exceptions to this, such as a previously independent person suffering a devastating stroke with no prospect of a return to independent living.

Just as there are shock/horror stories from time to time about care homes, so there are with hospitals. As well as some concerns about patients' dignity, the main complaints appear to be lack of proper food and staff not helping immobile patients to eat. Much of this may be media hype. Food is never 'withheld' from dying patients – they often do not wish to eat or are unable to eat, which is different. Stopping eating and drinking is very common in the final stages of illness; there is no evidence that this causes any suffering, provided the mouth is kept moist.

Many wards may welcome the offer of family members coming in to assist at mealtimes if a patient is unable to feed themselves. Ask the staff. They won't let relatives cut toenails while a patient is in hospital – quite apart from the fact that other patients don't want to see it, there's a risk of injury and infection, especially if the patient is diabetic. Filing of fingernails is not an issue, however.

Relatives spending hours and hours by a bedside can be a nuisance and get in the nursing staff's way, but in certain situations hospitals will try to allow relatives 24/7, for example with terminally ill patients or people who don't speak any English. Staff will try and be sympathetic and accommodating if there is a good reason.

And talking of staff ... people do like to be thanked, and it certainly helps the general atmosphere to be polite to them and not complain and moan all the time. Try to keep a sense of humour. Incidentally, although much is made of 'patient feedback', the forms are often not completed.

Hospices

One comment everyone makes is how wonderful hospices are. They are excellent organisations to support if you are looking to do voluntary work in your area. Contrary to what many people think, they are not just for cancer patients and they are not only for dying in – lots of people go into a hospice for a couple of weeks of symptom control and then go back home or into the NHS system.

Funding

Statistics indicate that the average person may be in a care home for two years at a cost of around £25,000 a year, but for wealthier people, who tend to be in better health, the figures are four years at £50,000 or so per year. Just over 10% of us may be in a care home for eight years. We are not talking small sums, therefore, and it is no wonder that there is endless debate about how much we should or shouldn't contribute to our care costs.

Under a scheme called 'Direct Payments' your needs are assessed by a social worker, then the local authority funds care costs, as well as paying for advertising for the carer that you want to employ. If you don't want the hassle of choosing/employing your own carer, you can use the money to pay an agency. But currently this scheme may be of limited usefulness for frail older people because, even with assistance, they may not have the skills to commission their own package of care. This will probably change as today's middle-aged people grow older and become more demanding about their rights and personal choices.

If your assets, including the value of your home, are over a certain amount – currently just over

£20,000 according to where you live in the UK – you will have to pay the full cost of your accommodation and personal care. If your savings and assets are less than a certain amount, which again will vary according to where you live (currently £14,250 in England for example) the state will pay all costs. If you have capital between the two stipulated figures you will be expected to make some contribution – for every £250 you own you may be assessed as if you have an extra £1 per week of income. As your capital diminishes, this levy should drop each time you fall into a lower £250 band.

Sources of funding for your care include your state retirement pension, private income or pension, an annuity, Attendance Allowance, the NHS and the local authority, plus possibly the sale of your property. How generous your funding is may depend on how strapped authorities are at the time. Sometimes you might feel you need to be a juggler or a magician.

Don't be too proud to apply for any benefits for which you are eligible. Local authorities will assume you are receiving these when making their assessments. Some local authorities have been known to shade the figures to keep their costs down, estimating the cost of care at artificially low rates when means testing those who have run out of capital, and then refusing further help.

Some care homes may subsidise council-funded places by charging private residents more (perhaps up to 30% more) for the same service. Care in a retirement property may be similar, although there may be costs built into the service charge to cover on-site staff.

Summary of points when considering a home

● Are the fees acceptable to you? Prices may vary quite widely between homes. Select somewhere you will be able to afford in the long term.

● Are the fees acceptable to your local authority, if they will be helping with the costs?

● It may be wise to consult the local authority early in your planning process; it may be more responsive if you have done so. Local authorities will have maximum amounts they will be prepared to pay. If you want the en-suite bathroom and the wine cellar you or a relative may have to meet the difference.

'The game's up – they've found the tunnel.'

- Any top-up contribution you are asked to make will depend upon your income, savings and any other assets you may have. Means testing about these matters is currently a subject of fierce debate.

- If you have deliberately given away assets to prevent them being included in the local authority's assessment, they may still be treated as if you still owned them. And they may regard a mad spending spree in a ploy to reduce your assets as a deliberate act to avoid paying. Take care!

- Although it is often convenient for couples to have joint bank accounts, it may in fact be better to have separate ones, because local authorities do not have the right to use a spouse's assets to fund care for their partner.

- Also under debate is whether your former home should be included as part of your capital. It should certainly be ignored if your stay in a care home is only temporary, or if a spouse or partner still lives in it, or any other relative who is either over 60 or receiving disability benefit.

- If a home is above the authority's funding limit but there are no other suitable homes available then the authority should be prepared to pay the extra. Get things in writing, and perhaps have a relative or friend vet any contract for you so that you are absolutely clear on what is or isn't included in the fees, and what you may be charged for any extras.

- Be aware of what charges will apply if you are away in hospital for a spell, as well as what notice you will need to give if you wish to leave the home. It's also worth checking if any charges will be made if you die while in residence.

- If a resident runs out of capital (total asset value, not just cash), except for the sum which current legislation allows, a social services and local authority panel will assess future funding needs and how these can be met.

- Finally, when you die, funeral costs and arrangements are generally the responsibility of the family.

Coping as a carer

● Recognise that you are, in fact, a carer. You may have drifted into it and not realised that it has become a full-time role.

● If you are the sole carer of someone who depends on you, carry some sort of note to that effect with you in case – heaven forbid – you get knocked down while just nipping to the shops. Social services can arrange emergency support, but they need to know there is a vulnerable person on their own.

● Consider your own needs, or you won't be able to carry out your role as a carer properly. Try to find some 'me' time. Caring for a terminally ill person can be stressful, but if that results in days when it all seems a bit too much, the patient will usually understand and take it in their stride because they will know the feeling all too well.

● Don't transfer your own problems to the person you are caring for.

● If you are caring for someone you don't know, take the trouble to find out something about them so that you have common ground for conversation.

● This is not a chapter for professional carers, whose employers will be responsible for their training. Most informal carers will already have some form of relationship with the patient, whether as a relative or friend, but if the circumstances are different then establish how the patient would prefer to be addressed. Someone who has been called 'Sir' all their business life may not appreciate a 'Hello, Alf' approach. And while on nomenclature, not everyone will want to be called a 'patient', which I've used here for simplicity. One label won't fit everyone.

● Establish clear guidelines on responsibilities and, if you are not a relative, be clear about liaison with those who are. This assumes, of course, that the patient actually wants their relatives involved; they have no automatic entitlement to any information.

If you are caring for someone you don't know, take the trouble to find out something about them so that you have common ground for conversation.

- Care needs to be prioritised so that time is not wasted. Patients have to feel well cared for, but it's also important for a carer to have a feeling of a job well done. List what you do for them, and if they need more help than you are able to give, find the appropriate professional.

- Avoiding mutual embarrassment over toiletry? By the time someone requires help they are likely to be beyond being embarrassed about it. Just explain what you are doing and check that the person is comfortable with that and, if not, ask what you can do better. Ensure bathroom doors are not left wide open and make the area as private as possible to maintain the person's dignity. And ensure you've got all the things to hand before you start – gloves, pads, toilet paper, clean pants and so on.

- Sadly, you may need to consider your own safety, because dementia may lead to physical violence towards medical staff and carers; seeking help on such occasions does not make you a failure as a carer. In fact, violence is not the commonest health and safety issues for carers. Moving and handling patients can be very hard work for both them and you, while just plain mental and physical exhaustion may become an issue.

- On a wider front, if necessary alert a person you care for to the risk of safety issues like bogus callers. The better rapport you have with the person you are caring for, the easier you will find such conversations without distressing them.

- If you are not a relative, don't get caught in family fights over patients. Also try to avoid them, for that matter, even if you are part of the family – you will all probably still be around when the patient isn't.

- Research what help is available such as grants and support from organisations run by counties and charities.

- The best of intentions may be misunderstood, especially on financial matters. Of course it makes sense for people to make Wills and be given sound financial advice, but come on too strong with suggestions in these areas and your motives may be misinterpreted. Ask if they want advice before barging in. If someone has a beloved pet, they may wish to leave money to a charity relating to it – try not to interfere by suggesting the money should go to medical care or whatever you think would be appropriate instead. It's not your call.

- Communication is important, and although it is impossible to generalise, check if you need to face patients so that they can lip-read. Try to avoid having to shout because this can cause tension. In some cases it may be helpful to have pictures or photographs that can be pointed at, to help with clear communication. Several products – including tracking devices – are available to let you stay in touch with someone you are caring for even when you're not in the room with them. Baby monitors are widely used, which may sound belittling, but they're only intercoms after all.

- If your patient can sometimes be disruptive, at the cinema say, then perhaps take them to matinees or morning showings; these are more geared to the older generation who may be more tolerant than an evening audience.

Caring or keeping an eye on someone

- If several friends or relatives are sharing the caring then liaise via a simple rota to avoid confusion or duplicated effort, or even a growing resentment that 'I'm doing all the work'. This will also reassure the patient, through having regular company.

- A photo-montage by the patient's bed, of incidents in their life or places they liked to visit, may act as a useful prompt if conversation flags.

Seek professional guidance. No unpaid carer should be managing a bed-bound patient without the right help and equipment.

- If possible, have just one of the caring team making contact with the hospital or care home, otherwise there could be confusion. Doctors will not have time to speak to umpteen friends or relatives individually, and it is not unreasonable for a doctor to tell only one person and expect them to share the information.

- Although medical or caring staff should invite involved family/friends to care planning meetings, when it is important to ensure everyone is in the picture and able to contribute opinions, they will not have time to invite them to every case conference. If you are invited to attend, don't let your concerns make you pugnacious. Patients can become demanding and crotchety. Don't add to the tension.

- Try to establish a good working relationship with staff. A 'not them moaning again' reputation is unlikely to produce the best results. Yes, there are cases of neglect and abuse, but they are rarer than the media sometimes suggest. Most professional carers do care, and a lot of the neglect reported in the media is as a result of being stretched and busy, not a wilful desire to be nasty.

- Have direct contact with the treating team if possible – the nurses, who may be more readily available, and ward-based junior doctors, not just the consultant. And remember there may be no one available at the very instant that you want to talk to them, so you may quite reasonably be told 'No, not now', with an alternative time suggested. All too often the relatives who complain that not everything is being done quickly and correctly for their loved one are the same ones who want to talk to someone every day for ages … with no thought for the fact that the time they are taking up means less time for patients!

- If you feel that things are going awry then keep a 'war diary' so that you have evidence to back up any argument you wish to make.

- Bed sores in someone you are caring for? Seek professional guidance. No unpaid carer should be managing a bed-bound patient without the right help and equipment. Simple preventatives like maintaining mobility – even if this is just standing up every hour or so – is all carers should do without advice.

- Avoid lifting people. This won't stop people doing so, but it is not advised.

- It may be harrowing to read of doctors prescribing water to ensure patients get enough, although such cases are very rare. But it is not unreasonable for carers to ask wards what measures are in place; for example, some may have red trays to indicate those who need assistance with feeding.

- Carers (and relatives, of course) should communicate with medical staff in a timely manner. They aren't mind readers so, for instance, don't write down a list of problems, smile at the ward staff as you leave and say nothing … and then write a letter of complaint. Talk to staff, giving them a chance to correct or explain things.

- If you are struggling with your carer role and your loved one is admitted to hospital then tell the staff at the beginning of the admission, and try to be clear about what specifically you are struggling with. Don't wait to be told the patient is ready to go home, then throw in the towel and say: 'They can't come home, I can't cope.'

- If you have had enough and simply cannot continue your carer role – fair enough, it happens – be honest with the patient and tell them that. All too often people tell staff they can't cope but shy away from being honest with their loved one. Doctors can't plan an alternative with the patient if they are sitting there thinking 'my daughter will do it'.

Caring for those with Alzheimer's

Dementia can present particular problems for relatives, not least in watching the decline of a loved one.

- Try to delay 'closedown' as long as possible. Aim to keep sufferers cheerful and active. Singing with them may be helpful and if nothing else may cheer them up, unless, of course, your own singing is particularly painful – although that may make them laugh!

- Gently prompt them if they have forgotten something.

- Don't ask them direct questions or contradict them.

- Focus on what they can do rather than on what they can't.

- Don't speak too quickly or use long sentences if they are having difficulty understanding.

- Keep in mind that sufferers can put themselves in danger because they don't appreciate the risks of traffic or a hot stove.

- Be aware of signs like restlessness, meaning they need the toilet.

- All sorts of visual aids may help, such as pictures to go on doors, particularly if in unfamiliar places, or bold colours for cutlery or special crockery. As with all these things, though, one suggestion will not suit all.

Support for carers

It is estimated that there are over six million informal carers in the UK, so you are not alone. There is a range of practical and emotional support available.

- Charities devoted to a particular condition are likely to have advice for those caring for sufferers.

- There may be online forums where carers can compare experiences and perhaps be kept up to date with developments, although be a shade wary of reports of new wonder treatments because they may not be suitable or available for all.

- Visit www.carersuk.org where you will find help.

- Trawl local council offices and libraries for information for older people and their carers. You should find information on what is available and who is eligible for assistance with home food deliveries, shopping services, home adaptations and repairs, and many other services.

- Link into any local carer support groups and consider some respite care (see www.nhs.uk/ CarersDirect).

- Don't forget to ask for professional advice where necessary. People can waste hundreds of pounds on electric beds, mobility chairs, etc. that are completely unsuitable for their particular needs.

- Finally, carers may well be concerned that they will see their patient or relative die. People react differently on such occasions, but from personal experience I know that witnessing a death can be a most moving and uplifting experience.

Contract

wer of attorney

Testament

MORTGAGE LOAN AGREEME

ARTICLE I   2

Definitions

Section 1.1   Definitions ....

ARTICLE II   6

Pledge; Control and Perfection   7

Section 2.1   The Pledge ....
Section 2.2   Control and Perfection

ARTICLE III

LEGAL AFFAIRS

Wills

I'll use a capital W for Will to avoid any confusion with sentences like 'If I make a will, will I feel happier?' You can, of course, make your own Will using standard forms available in stationers, while many banks provide a Wills service. And there are Will-writing companies; some are good, some are not so good. Beware of being talked into 'extras' that you don't really need.

If a Will is badly written it can cause endless stress and cost to your beneficiaries so, if you can afford it, it is better to forge a link with a solicitor. You may, of course, have other legal issues for which a solicitor will be useful. Word of mouth is the best way of finding a solicitor or use *Yellow Pages*, the internet or the Law Society website (www.lawsociety.org.uk) to find a firm in your area. Make sure they specialise in Wills – not all firms of solicitors do nowadays. It can be helpful to have a solicitor some years younger than you are, so that he or she is likely to be around when your affairs are finally wound up.

The law says that a Will must be in writing (so no video Wills yet). It must be signed by the person making it in the presence of two witnesses, and everyone should sign in everyone else's presence. A beneficiary cannot be a witness. That all sounds very simple, but people have an amazing capacity for making a mess of those instructions. The law is very strict on the issue and your beneficiaries may not find out it's wrong until it's too late and you're six feet under.

Only around a third of us make Wills, perhaps because people think death won't happen to them. That is undoubtedly an over-optimistic approach. But if you don't make a Will the intestacy rules will apply when you die and may produce results you wouldn't have wanted. If friends or relatives are reluctant to make Wills, it may help concentrate their minds to suggest that if they don't then Mr X (insert here the name of their least favourite government minister) may have a say in what happens to their assets.

Making your Will

- Making a Will means you can protect your relatives and ensure your assets go where you would have wanted. And you can choose as executors those people you know will carry out your wishes.

- Make sure you understand charges in advance, including those for dealing with the 'probate', which is the legal term for sorting it all out when you are no longer around. Remember that solicitors will charge for being executors, although in practice the charges may come out at no more for them acting as your executor than if they didn't: having a solicitor with control over the whole procedure may actually speed things up.

- The more complicated your affairs, the greater reason to make a Will:

  - Making a Will may help in avoiding inheritance tax (IHT).
  - Not least, making a Will can give you peace of mind in knowing it's all sorted.

- Resist the temptation to use a Will as a 'weapon' to buy affection.

- Getting married invalidates any previous Will. You can make a Will 'in contemplation of marriage', where there is a specific marriage to a specific person at a specific date lined up, thus making provision for a fiancée, and that won't be revoked. But that one example apart, any earlier Will is invalid.

- You can change a Will by drawing up a codicil, i.e. a simple note to add to or alter the contents of a Will. This must be treated in the same way as the full Will outlined above, i.e. by the person making the Will signing in the presence of two witnesses and so forth. If there have been major changes in your life, it is probably better to make an entirely new Will.

- Solicitors will provide a bedside Will service for someone dying or otherwise unable to visit them.

- If you do not want a particular person to benefit when you die, you may need to spell this out very specifically because courts have the power to make provision for your dependants if you yourself fail to make 'reasonable provision' for them. This applies not only to spouses and children who were dependants but also a partner (of either sex) who was financially dependent.

Make sure you understand charges in advance, including those for dealing with the 'probate', which is the legal term for sorting it all out when you are no longer around.

- What you may not be able to prevent is a Deed of Variation after you have died under which, if the beneficiaries agree, the terms of a Will can be altered, for instance to skip a generation for inheritance tax reasons. This is not difficult to do, although it may in fact go against what the deceased actually wanted. These Deeds of Variation were introduced way back in the 1930s to make provision for those who genuinely should have been provided for, such as a spouse or a child, or where the law of intestacy was going to leave a spouse on hard times. The wording of the legislation was arguably a bit loose and it was soon realised that the same legislation could be used for tax planning purposes as well. But let's not knock it – there isn't much tax planning left to us these days (at least any that's legal), so let's hang on to what we've got.

- Many charities offer a free service for preparing a basic Will if you are intending to leave them something – not surprising, considering that some charities receive half their income from legacies. Money left to charities is exempt from inheritance tax, provided the wording in the Will is correct. And it doesn't have to be money you leave to a charity – it can be property, paintings or other valuables. But beware of leaving so much to charity that your dependants feel hurt enough to take court action. Charities may be legally bound to contest such actions in order to fight for anything left to them. Legal costs could then mean both sides suffering. Keep in mind that charities are run as businesses nowadays, so they may want every last penny they can extract out of any legacy, especially if they are left a share of the residuary estate.

- Be sure you have the correct names for beneficiaries, whether individuals or charities.

- With high levels of divorce today, you may not be keen to leave things to a married child in case their marriage breaks up and some of 'your' assets end up going to a disliked son- or daughter-in-law. A pre-nuptial agreement may solve this, although insisting on one may not do anything for your relationship with your child and their future marriage partner. Consider leaving assets to your child in trust instead.

133

On the death of someone, those left behind may find it beneficial to have professional help when valuing the deceased's estate in order to reduce any tax payable.

- It is common practice for couples to make very similar or even identical Wills, perhaps leaving everything to each other before it all passes to children or grandchildren on the death of the second partner. However, the second person to die could, of course, change their minds and alter their Will. It might be safer to spell out in the first of such Wills that they are 'mutual Wills', in which case the survivor cannot alter the main provisions. The law is very pedantic about this and it's definitely a situation for consulting a solicitor to get the wording right. It must be quite clear (at a later date) that there was an intention that the Wills should be mutual and that intention can be proved.

- Many couples own property on a 'joint tenants' basis, under which a surviving partner will automatically own the whole of the property irrespective of what is in your Will. However, if instead you own somewhere on a 'tenants in common' basis, each of you can specify in your Will who is to get your share of the property on your death.

- On the death of someone, those left behind may find it beneficial to have professional help when valuing the deceased's estate in order to reduce any tax payable.

- Most solicitors will not charge a fee for holding a copy of your Will. If you keep a copy at home, don't leave it where anyone can get access to it, although make sure at least one trusted person knows where it is.

    There is now a National Will Register which, for a small fee, will record the existence of your Will and where it is held; this is becoming popular as it is sensible to make it easier for people to track down the whereabouts of your Will when you are no longer around to tell them.

- Trusts are a possible means of protecting property in the future, e.g. protecting assets for your children in case they take to gambling or drinking, or marrying unwisely, etc.; preserving assets for your children in the event of your spouse remarrying; or simply preserving flexibility to apply assets in the future in the most practical and/or tax efficient manner at that time. Trusts fall under very complicated legal and tax regulations, however, and they are not a DIY job or something to be done lightly. Get specialist advice.

Power of Attorney

- As well as making a Will, it makes eminent sense to draw up a Power of Attorney nominating friends or relatives and authorising them to act in your place if you become incapable. Such a legal agreement can make things a great deal easier for your nearest and dearest should the need arise.

- Although at first sight they can seem complicated, Powers of Attorney are not really so and are worth doing. Don't leave it too late to implement one. 'Enduring Power of Attorney' is now a redundant term in the sense that you can't make one now (but a Lasting Power of Attorney instead) but there are still lots of EPAs around and they are still valid for financial matters. Some doctors have yet to see a patient with an LPA because the law has only been in place since 2007 and you would have had to have mental capacity to make one, so most of the early uptake of the new LPA will still have their faculties and the LPA will still be in reserve for when they 'lose it'.

* The idea of a Lasting Power of Attorney is that the person/s nominated know you well enough to work out what you would want in the circumstances in which you find yourself. In England and Wales a Lasting Power of Attorney is one of two types – a Property and Affairs LPA, to cover your finances, and a Personal Welfare LPA, embracing your health and welfare. The first covers all your assets, the second covers your welfare and could, for instance, decide if you need to be in a care home; there is sufficient flexibility to give pretty clear guidance on what kind of medical help you would or would not approve of in different situations, although in reality it's a lot easier said than done. You can make just one of them or, better, both and you

can have a different attorney for each if you wish – you may decide that one person would make good decisions on your behalf regarding your health but would be rubbish with money, or vice versa. Or you can nominate more than one person and also decide if they can act on an either/or basis or that both have to agree on a decision taken on your behalf.

- Things are different in Scotland where there is a Continuing Power of Attorney for your finance and a Welfare one for your health; as in England and Wales, you can do the two together.

- You will have to get a certificate from someone unconnected with the nominated attorneys to certify that you have the mental capacity to understand that you are handing over power to those attorneys; the certificate has to be from someone of good standing who has known you for a minimum of two years.

- A Lasting Power of Attorney has to be registered with the Office of the Public Guardian or the Office of the Public Guardian (Scotland), with a fee of £130 for each currently payable. (Scots have a better deal because their fee is only just over half that, whether you have one or two parts registered.) Get something wrong, by the way, and you have to pay all over again, which is an argument for taking professional advice.

- The registration has to be done while you still have sufficient mental capacity. In theory, the attorneys could then start acting for you, but in most cases the document is filed and only activated when you start to decline. In practice your attorneys, acting in tandem with your GP, are likely to be the ones who decide when this point has been reached.

- Many Powers of Attorney are done between partners, giving each authority to look after the other's finance or welfare, but it is important that other attorneys are appointed – this is quite often a son or daughter (or two) – not least because partners may decline in 'harmony'.

Living Wills

- These can be drawn up to record what treatment you want if you are dying under an end-of-life charter.

- Advanced Directives or Living Wills can be legally formalised, but doctors are required to take them into account even if they are just written on a scrap of paper or merely verbally reported to someone. Doctors do have to be as sure as they can be, however, that the individual was of sound mind when leaving the instruction, so a formal approach is really better. The advantage of an Advanced Directive is that it is then absolutely clear what you do or do not want. The disadvantage is that it is virtually impossible to predict all the permutations that may happen and how you will feel at the time. As an example, the idea of needing help to wash, dress and use the toilet may be abhorrent now from the perspective of an able-bodied person, but who knows what our capacity to adjust might be should anything happen to us? In this context 'value statements' are more useful than 'if X happened I would/would not want Y'.

- Personally I want to leave my body to science but the scientists keep contesting the Will.

Additional information

- As well as a Will and a Power of Attorney, you should consider creating a 'Letter of wishes' (or statement of wishes) complementing your Will to indicate how you want your executor/s to use their discretion in settling your estate, for instance in who should receive specific personal items or even perhaps to explain why someone should not receive something. (Valuable things of course should be left to people in your Will or be sold by your executor to be part of your estate.)

- Either as part of this letter of wishes or as yet another document, you should leave details of such things as:
  - Where credit card statements are kept.

Although at first sight they can seem complicated, Powers of Attorney are not really so and are worth doing. Don't leave it too late to implement one.

– User names, passwords and PIN numbers – but only with care. Don't include such information in an actual Will because this may be open to public inspection and your accounts could be raided.
– Anything – cash or other items – borrowed or owed. Any object you'd like to go to a particular person. You may decide not to mention any.

● Standing orders which may need cancelling.

● Drawing up a list like this:

– Eases the strain on those left.
– Helps prevent family squabbles.
– Stops valuable things being thrown out. If you have an esoteric hobby, something weird or small may be very valuable but people may not know this unless you leave a note saying so.

● Such a list can be combined with, or at least kept in the same place as, an outline of your wishes for your funeral.

Euthanasia

● This is one of the greatest ethical and legal issues of the day. Some argue that 'It's my body, I'll do what I like with it', while others find this attitude abhorrent.

● A growing number of elderly people want to end their lives when they wish, even if they are not terminally ill when they decide to do so. They tend to be strong-willed people who don't relish the idea of others deciding what is or isn't good for them.

● Two-thirds of us now believe that someone who is terminally ill but of sound mind should be allowed the option of ending their life, avoiding 'prolonged dwindling' and a life with more pain than pleasure.

● There is plenty of information – some would say too much information – about euthanasia and suicide available online.

● Whatever the law, society needs to protect the vulnerable from being 'encouraged' to die by people with dubious reasons, whether simply to make their own lives easier by not having to continue a caring role, or for direct financial gain. Conversely, people helping others to die for entirely honourable reasons should not face prosecution (although this seems to be becoming increasingly less likely anyway).

● Certainly, for those who believe in euthanasia, it should not be necessary to take a flight to Switzerland to end their life. I've nothing against that country, but who wants an airline sandwich as their last meal?

● Keep in mind that while being killed by a poison is currently illegal in the UK, it is perfectly legal, and perhaps preferable, for a compos mentis person to tell their doctors that they've had enough: they don't want the latest suggested treatment to prolong life, opting instead for a 'keep comfortable, symptom control only' approach.

Cohabiting couples

● Cohabiting couples have no specific legal rights over a property they share if they split up, even if there are children involved. 'Common law wife' has no meaning in law, and nor has 'common law husband'.

● This could mean disaster if, say, a partner leaves with most of the assets in his (or her) name, rendering the other person penniless. It is still the case that people 'living together' and wanting to be sure about the future of their assets should take legal advice.

● The rise in the number of couples voluntarily deciding to live together without benefit of clergy or registrar must inevitably lead to clearer laws on this issue in the future, but until then it is vital to discuss how to divide assets if you split up and then, preferably, visit a solicitor together. The safest thing is to draw up a trust deed or cohabitation agreement, setting out in clear detail who owned what when the couple set up home together. Such discussions hardly come into the romantic 'moonlight and roses' category, but a look at the statistics makes them seem wise.

Two-thirds of us now believe that someone who is terminally ill but of sound mind should be allowed the option of ending their life.

Try to keep your temper, although this may not be easy if you've listened to 20 minutes of music while waiting for a customer service line to answer.

- A surviving partner may inherit nothing unless they have been specifically provided for in a Will.

Same-sex partnerships

- Same-sex partners who have a proper civil partnership, i.e. have had a legal civil partnership ceremony, are treated in the same way as a mixed-gender couple. So, for example, the death of the first of them will qualify for total tax exemption if the estate is bequeathed to the survivor.

- There are some inequalities. Unlike a married couple, a surviving partner will not benefit from their partner's public sector pension, so it's important to see whether your pension provider will let you sign a nomination form in which you tell them who you want to benefit from your pension pot if you die before collecting it yourself.

- Also worth considering is whether a same-gender partner would have a claim as a 'dependant' of the deceased if there is no Will, or a Will that does not leave financial provision for that partner.

Other legal issues

- The saddest legal stories in the media are of feuds between neighbours, with huge legal costs incurred in a dispute over a tiny boundary or, literally, a pile of horse manure. The next time you see an idiotic case reported in a newspaper, cut it out, and you and your neighbours sign the cutting and agree that you will never let such lunacy happen to you. Digging the document out may, just may, stop the red mist coming down over an issue in the future. Mediation will invariably be a whole lot cheaper than a court case; some courts, in fact, may insist on mediation being tried first. But just in case, check if any insurance you have will cover an issue.

- Age discrimination? Don't put up with it!

- If, sadly, you have to fight for access to grandchildren it may help to have solicitors guiding you. Make sure the firm is a specialist in family law and not just a generalist.

- Today's blame culture means that 'somebody must pay', so I guess we are all more likely to become involved in litigation. If it is a major issue affecting a lot of people there will almost certainly be an online campaign launched. Join it.

- If you enter into a 'no win/no fee' arrangement, be quite clear what, if any, contribution may in fact be expected from you (this may be hidden in the small print) and be equally clear what percentage of any 'winnings' will actually come to you.

- Persevere if you have a complaint about a company or organisation. Write to a particular person if you can identify one. Don't waffle; keep letters concise and to the point.

- Try to keep your temper, although this may not be easy if you've listened to 20 minutes of music while waiting for a customer service line to answer.

- If you are unhappy with the service you have received from a solicitor you can complain to the firm's client care partner or manager. If you are still dissatisfied, then contact the Solicitors Regulation Authority. If you have chosen your legal adviser with care – perhaps at the suggestion of friends – this should not be necessary.

- Finally, these are complex issues which regularly change so, having decided which bits of the above apply to you and what you think you need to do, take professional advice. You should only need to do it once and it will help you to sleep – though preferably not while the solicitor is talking.

137

THE FINAL CURTAIN

Although you still see some mild competition to be the last to die, with people checking the obituaries before getting up in the morning, attitudes are getting more relaxed, with people accepting that death – which has been described as Nature's way of telling us to slow down – is a natural part of life.

This has also led to a growing move towards less traditional funerals. Nowadays some 15% are non-religious, conducted by a celebrant rather than a religious body. I've even heard of someone who, as a supporter of recycling and a keen animal lover, wanted to be fed to the lions in a zoo. He changed his mind when his vicar pointed out the posthumous embarrassment he'd feel if the lions sniffed … and then refused to eat.

You can, of course, be buried in your own back garden. In fact, one funeral director reports doing one of these ceremonies roughly every five years. You don't need planning permission to be buried on your own land, just approval from the Environment Agency to prevent pollution of watercourses etc. You can only bury one person per garden, and maybe you also need to consider the effect on the price of the house when your next-of-kin try to sell it.

Many traditional cemeteries are under space pressure and it seems inevitable that there will have to be more recycling of old graves. After 75 years graves may be reused, with any remains exhumed and buried deeper to allow room for fresh burials – the 'lift-and deepen' system. Some cemeteries are burying 12ft deep at the moment so that plots can be used again in years to come.

If space pressures continue, it may be necessary to put the new-born child down for a burial plot at the same time as they are entered for a school. One friend bought a plot several years ago, decided to be cremated instead, and was then pleasantly surprised to sell the plot at a profit.

But whatever the trends, most people are likely to opt for a conventional funeral. Prices vary according to region but it is never a cheap operation. You only get one go at it, so it is worth some thought.

Deciding what you want

- You may feel that once you are dead it doesn't matter what sort of funeral you have. Others may have firmer ideas. The more that is settled in advance, the less strain there will be on the next-of-kin who will otherwise have to decide everything, so if possible discuss with the people likely to be involved or at least leave a note about what you would like. Unfortunately only around a third of people broach the subject, but you may care to discuss with close ones the details of your final days:

- Where would you like to die? Home or hospital?
- Do you want cremation or burial? If cremation, have you any specific wishes about what should happen to your ashes?
- Is there anything you would or would not like if you become either unable to understand important medical decisions or unable to communicate your wishes?

– Is there anyone you would like with you when you die? Perhaps equally importantly, is there anyone you would not want near you when you die?

– Have you anything you want to say to people, or any messages to be left for them?

And as regards the funeral itself, the following questions need to be considered:

● Where do you want the service to be held? Where you live or where you used to live? (Webcasting of funerals is, of course, possible so that people can 'participate' without actually being there; this is useful when friends or relatives have moved to other countries.)

● Is there anyone you would like to speak at your funeral? Or you could write an address yourself and ask someone to read it out on your behalf.

● Would you prefer any particular readings or hymns? Only around 40% of us leave a note of any wishes – it should be 100% to avoid confusion or unintentional merriment. The congregation was half way through singing 'How Great Thou Art' at one funeral I attended before recalling that the deceased had weighed 28 stone. 'Sheep May Safely Graze' was deliberately chosen by a butcher and the congregation smiled as they sang and remembered his keen sense of humour.

● Have you any thoughts about a dress code? A service I will never forget was for someone who stipulated that men should wear tasteless ties not black ones.

● Flowers and/or donations or nothing? Well over half of funerals ask for donations with, increasingly, 'family flowers only' stipulated. There doesn't seem to be much difference in the amount donated whether the money is given by a cheque, via the undertaker or put in a box at the place of service. Note 'box', not plate – I find it difficult to credit, but it has been known for money to be taken from, not added to, a plate. Not so easy with a box with a slot!

'You won't be needing that where we're going, sir.'

● Any special requests? As examples, I have heard of people stipulating that their hearse should pause outside a favourite pub or be driven along a particular road on the way to the service. One friend even stipulated that the hearse carrying his coffin should hit a highly illegal speed on a local motorway while en route – a classic example of thinking outside the box, perhaps?

● If you specifically do not want a memorial service you should leave instructions to that effect. Some next of kin find such services can be an added strain, while others find them heart-warming.

The funeral director

Anyone can arrange a funeral, although the local planning and health and safety people would have to be told what you were doing. It's better, if possible, to use an undertaker or funeral director

Have you any thoughts about a dress code? A service I will never forget was for someone who stipulated that men should wear tasteless ties not black ones.

(as they are now more commonly called) who is a member of NAFD (the National Association of Funeral Directors) or SAIF (the National Society of Allied and Independent Funeral Directors). They will handle everything the next-of-kin don't wish to do themselves, including printing an order of service, putting a notice in the newspaper of your choice, catering arrangements and even going with them to request the death certificate.

Most undertakers will have a funeral planning checklist which will guide you through the various stages of what has to be done in order for a funeral to take place plus details of who to tell that the loved one has died – bank, taxman, local council, etc. Fortunately, to simplify things, almost all councils in England have signed up to the 'Tell Us Once' service for births and deaths under which, once you have informed your local registrar, the information is shared – with your permission – across all the other organisations which may need to know, including councils, social services, libraries and so on.

The Medical Certificate is usually issued by the doctor who certified death, although it may not be possible for a doctor to issue a certificate if the death was caused by an accident or industrial disease, was sudden or perhaps violent, or occurred during an operation. In such cases the coroner will be informed and may order a post mortem. Relatives don't have to give their

approval for this to happen, but they can choose to have a doctor present on their behalf.

If the post mortem shows that death was due to natural causes then the coroner will issue a Pink Form for the registrar. If the cause of death remains uncertain the coroner may decide to hold an inquest.

The Medical Certificate or Pink Form should be taken to the local Registrar of Births and Deaths for the death to be registered. Full details of date and place of birth of the deceased plus maiden name will be needed. The registrar will then formally register the death and issue a Green Form for the undertaker. If there is no living kin then it could be left to the council or the solicitor to arrange matters, but if a Will requested that a best mate or the executor was going to arrange the funeral then the doctor would give the form to them.

Don't assume nursing home or care home staff will know the drill – staff may be foreign and used to different customs. It's always better to have someone who knows the ropes on board. Many crematoriums are busy, so local undertakers tend to liaise over diaries in order that things run smoothly. If arranging a cremation for a popular character who is likely to attract a large number of mourners, consider booking two consecutive slots at the crematorium (although some now allow 40 minutes, which is enough for most services).

'You have reached your destination.'

Whether it is your funeral you are planning or that for someone else, it helps to meet the undertakers well before you need their services. Even being able to put a face to a name may help at a time of grief.

Obtain at least two quotes from undertakers, being careful to compare like with like, although it can be such an emotional time that their approach and understanding may be more important than their price. Bear in mind that it is not unknown for under-the-counter payments to be made to nursing homes, or even doctors, so try to establish that any advice you are given is impartial.

Burial charges are going up – tactless, I thought, of someone to say it's because of the increased cost of living – and may include fees for church, doctor, removal of pacemaker, crematorium, gravediggers, printed service sheets, flowers, obituary notices, coffin or casket, organist, churchyard burial fee, catering, etc., etc.

Bank accounts are frozen on death, until probate is granted, but a bank will pay invoices to do with the funeral if there is sufficient money in the account; however, they won't simply hand over the money. Those on low incomes may qualify for a means-tested grant from the social fund; the actual funeral service will seem 'normal' although the grant is unlikely to pay for any frills like flowers, and a local authority may seek to claim any assets to help cover their costs.

Incidentally, don't be surprised if a funeral director wishes to be clear on terms of payment; bad debt is quite a problem for the profession, partly I guess because they can't exactly reclaim the goods.

If you talk to the older generation they will recall how anxious people were to have proper funerals and how they would put money aside for them. Today, we have various payment-in-advance schemes. Around 10% of us take out such schemes, which are now government monitored to protect consumers. Be clear exactly what you have signed up for and ask any 'what happens if…?' questions that occur to you. As an example, undertakers may guarantee their own charges but not those of third parties, so if the cost of food trebles at the venue chosen for the wake you can hardly expect them to cover it. I think it is better to pay a lump sum rather

'I'm at work, can I ring you later?'

than take out an insurance scheme – if you have to pay the latter until you die you may find yourself in a situation where you can't afford to keep up the payments, so you will lose out.

Other things to arrange with the undertaker include whether the deceased is to be viewed in the coffin. Around 70% are. Mercifully, the American idea of drive-through viewing, where you can dial up which body you wish to view on a screen, has not taken hold.

The coffin

This is, of course, a key item:

● Customers can turn up with a home-made coffin if, say, the deceased was a carpenter. This will be OK for burial if it is sound. A crematorium may ask for two to be made; they may test one, then use the other on the day.

Customers can turn up with a home-made coffin if, say, the deceased was a carpenter. This will be OK for burial if it is sound.

- Coffins painted in, say, football club colours are being marketed and around 3% now take that form, although they are not cheap.

- The number of wicker coffins is heading for 10%, but 'going green' isn't cheap either.

- Inevitably the cost of all coffins will rise with increasing obesity, which is also leading to increased costs with crematoria having to be enlarged and fitted with bigger lifts and fridges.

- Most coffins are chipboard, with few now hand made in solid wood. It is, of course, a delicate matter of personal choice, but it is difficult to see the sense in an ornate solid wood coffin when nobody in the congregation will be able to tell the difference and the body will deteriorate whatever you do.

- Having decided on a coffin, you need a hearse. A motorcycle sidecar version may cost twice as much as a conventional hearse, with dashing white or black horses pulling a carriage at least double that again.

Vicars

A common comment after a funeral is that the vicar 'obviously didn't know the deceased'. If so, that is the fault of the next-of-kin, not the vicar. It is very helpful for a vicar, or whoever is taking the service (it doesn't have to be a priest), as it is for an undertaker, if people have written down in advance what they want at their funeral. This stops the bereaved feeling concerned that they may have got things wrong ... 'I don't know if Mum wanted to be buried or cremated.'

People are reluctant to discuss such things, but as we are all going to die it is far better to have things sorted. To that end, a vicar will encourage people to talk about their wishes; if someone is ill and facing death, a vicar would prefer to be able to visit them and talk to them about their lives, rather than to their next-of-kin when it is too late. It's not about converting them, but sharing that final journey with the family and building a relationship with them. In former times most people were known by their vicar because

Right: Coffins can come in all shapes and sizes as of course can their occupants.

www.crazycoffins.co.uk   (photo by Roger Bamber)

> The more open people have been and the more realistic in accepting that death is inevitable, the better they are likely to cope.

people lived in one parish, with one priest, but things are different today.

If the vicar hasn't met the deceased before they die then the family should produce some notes and biographical details. Better still, instead of leaving it to the vicar to pay tribute, have a close friend or family member do it – someone who knew the person so can talk with conviction.

Having now been privileged (and it really is a privilege) to be asked to pay tributes at some dozen funerals, I would suggest that if you are asked to do so you contact several friends of the deceased for their thoughts. If they all respond with a comment about, say, the deceased's sense of humour, then there's the theme for your tribute. I think it is worth clearing what you are going to say with a member of the family as well. If you feel you may break down in the emotion of the moment then give whoever is taking the service a copy of your words and ask them to step in and read the final paragraph or two if necessary. Knowing that someone has a spare copy will, in fact, probably give you the confidence to get through your panegyric.

As far as the rest of the service is concerned, a vicar will, or should, try to accommodate what the family wants. Some vicars may get a bit precious about what music or hymns can or cannot be used in 'their' church. But they are missing the point. A funeral may be one of the rare occasions when some people go into a church. If the experience is positive and welcoming they might just one day want to go back. It is, by the way, a mark of a good vicar, and funeral director too, if they can see 'My Way', 'All Things Bright and Beautiful' or 'Always Look on the Bright Side of Life' on service sheets five times in the same week without wincing.

Moving from the bier to the beer, invite the undertaker and the vicar to any wake. The family should be able to estimate the likely numbers who will attend, and if it is a local VIP then the undertaker may take a reasonable guess too. If you underestimated numbers, a quick phone call before the service starts may give the venue an extra hour for sandwich cutting.

Comforting the bereaved

People react to bereavement in different ways, but listening and talking to them may help at their time of grief. You can't stop people feeling sad, but giving them a shoulder to cry on may be a great comfort.

The more open people have been and the more realistic in accepting that death is inevitable, the better they are likely to cope. We tend to say 'let me know if I can do anything', but the bereaved may respond better to a more specific offer, such as help with funeral arrangements or asking if you should contact his golf club or her line-dancing friends or whatever. Even if the bereaved want to do all this themselves, they may still welcome advice and support. Further down the road, helping with house clearance may be welcomed, while if the grief is long lasting there may be local help groups to support them.

You may, of course, have to comfort children when someone has died. There are excellent children's bereavement charities available if you need guidance with this.

It may also help to talk to children about dying when a pet has to be put down so that they don't get false or exaggerated ideas. But still expect some unusual questions – be honest in your answers and if you don't know the answer then say so. (It may be important to tell a child's teacher of any death, as they may get questioned too.) It helps to use clear language – 'died' rather than 'passed away', for instance – while saying that you've 'lost' someone may suggest they may be found and return. It may help to encourage children to assemble some memorabilia about a loved one who has died.

Should children attend funerals? Yes, if they wish, although if it is their first funeral then brief them in advance about what will happen.

This is something of a sad chapter with which to end the book, but if someone has lived a full and rewarding life, with a happy retirement, then a well-planned funeral is a fitting conclusion.

FURTHER INFORMATION

The UK is fortunate in having many organisations to help with all kinds of ailments and misfortunes. The following are just some of them; the publisher would be happy to include others in future editions. Many of them are charities and some may have local branches where literature and help may be available. Websites rather than postal addresses are listed because most information is available online, avoiding postage; in some cases the information may be available only online.

Ability Net
www.itcanhelp.org.uk
Computer help for disabled people

Action Fraud
www.actionfraud.org.uk
National fraud reporting centre

Action on Hearing Loss
www.actiononhearingloss.org.uk
Support for people with hearing loss and tinnitus

Age UK
www.ageuk.org.uk
Wide range of help through information, advice, campaigns and products

Aidis Trust
www.aidis.org
Helping those with disabilities take advantage of computer technology

Alcoholics Anonymous
www.alcoholics-anonymous.org.uk
Primary purpose to stay sober and help other alcoholics to achieve sobriety

Al Anon
www.al-anonuk.org.uk
Support for anyone whose life is, or has been, affected by someone else's drinking

Allergy UK
www.allergyuk.org
Help for people with allergy, food intolerance and chemical sensitivity

Alzheimer's Society
www.alzheimers.org.uk
Supports people to live well with dementia today and funds research to find a cure for tomorrow

Arthritis Care
www.arthritiscare.org.uk
Supporting people with arthritis

Arthritis Research UK
www.arthritisresearch.uk.org
Funds research and has information on all types of arthritis

Beating Bowel Cancer
www.beatingbowelcancer.org
Information and support

Bladder and Bowel Foundation
www.bladderandbowelfoundation.org
Information and support

Blood donation
www.blood.co.uk
Comprehensive advice on giving blood

British Association for Counselling and Psychotherapy
www.bacp.co.uk
Setting standards for therapeutic practice

British Heart Foundation
www.bhf.org.uk
Information and support for those with a heart condition

Cancer Research UK
www.cancerresearchuk.org.
Research and information on all aspects of cancer

Care Quality Commission
www.cqc.org.uk
Inspects hospitals and care homes to ensure meeting government standards

Carers Direct
www.nhs.uk/carersrdirect
Information, advice and support for carers

Carers UK
www.carersuk.org
Help and advice for carers

Cinnamon Trust
www.cinnamon.org.uk
Support for the elderly, the terminally ill and their pets

Citizens Advice Bureau
www.citizensadvice.org.uk
Advice for people facing problems

Combat Stress
www.combatstress.org.uk
Military charity specialising in the care of veterans' mental health

Consumer Credit Counselling Service
www.cccs.co.uk
Assisting those in financial difficulty with free, impartial advice

Consumer Direct
www.consumerdirect.gov.uk
Consumer rights whether buying goods or services

Cosrt
www.cosrt.org.uk
Specialist charity for sexual and relationship therapy

Counsel and Care
www.counselandcare.org.uk
Advice service working with older people, their relatives and carers

Cruse Bereavement Care
www.crusebereavementcare.org.uk
Advice for the bereaved

Dementia web
www.dementiaweb.org.uk
All-age dementia information resource

Depression Alliance
www.depressionalliance.org
Information and support service

Diabetes UK
www.diabetes.org.uk
Care and support for all affected
by and at risk of diabetes.

**Diabetes Research & Wellness
Foundation**
www.drwf.org.uk
Supports, advises and educates
people with diabetes and the
general public

Directgov
www.direct.gov.uk
Public services all in one place

Disability Rights UK
www.disabilityalliance.org
Aims to be the largest national
pan-disability organisation led
by disabled people

Disabled Living Foundation
www.dlf.org.uk
Facts sheets on continence,
footwear, etc.

Disabled Motoring UK
www.disabledmotoring.org
Charity for disabled drivers,
passengers and Blue Badge holders

Do-it www.do-it.org.uk
Help for those who want
to volunteer

Drink Aware
www.drinkaware.co.uk
Helping people achieve the
right balance over alcohol

DVT Calculator
www.dvtcalculator.co.uk
Deep vein thrombosis risk assessment

Dying Matters
www.dyingmatters.org
Raising awareness of dying,
death and bereavement

Dying Matters coalition
www.dyingmatters.org
Encouraging people to talk about
their wishes towards the end

eBay
www.ebay.co.uk
Information on the online
market place

Elderly Accommodation Council
www.housingcare.org
Information on housing for
older people

Energy Saving Trust
www.energysavingtrust.org.uk
Advice on reducing carbon
emissions, using water sustainably
and saving money on energy bills

Epilepsy Society
www.epilepsysociety.org.uk
Medical charity working for
everyone affected by epilepsy

Forum of Mobility Centres
www.mobility-centres.org.uk
Information, advice, assessment

Friends at the End (Fate)
www.friends-at-the-end.org.uk
Promoting knowledge about
end-of-life choices and
dignified death

FSA Register
www.fsa.gov.uk/register
Public record of all firms and
individuals regulated by the
Financial Services Authority

General Dental Council
www.gdc-uk.org
Regulates dental professionals
in the UK

Get Safe Online
www.getsafeonline.org
Free independent advice on using
the internet safely and securely

Grandparents Association
www.grandparents-association.org.uk
Support for grandparents and
their families

Gransnet
www.gransnet.com
Social networking and
information for grandparents

HMRC
www.phishing@hmrc.gsi.gov.uk
Where to forward suspicious
emails about tax

Independent Living
www.independentliving.co.uk
Community website with news,
views and product information to
assist with living independently

**Institute of Cemetery and
Crematorium Management**
www.iccm-uk.com
Contact details for
bereavement services

International Glaucoma Association
www.glaucoma-association.com
Practical information and support

Jewish Care
www.jewishcare.org
Health and social care for the Jewish
community in London and the south-east

Jewish Deaf Association
www.jewishdeaf.org.uk
Independent national charity
offering support services
and information

Landlord & Buy-to-Let Magazine
www.landlordnet.co.uk
Free online/print magazine for
the private rented sector

Macmillan Cancer Support
www.macmillan.org.uk
Wide-ranging support for
those with cancer

Mailing Preference Service
www.mpsonline.org.uk
Where to get your name
removed from mailing lists

Marie Curie Cancer Care
www.mariecurie.org.uk
Providing care for terminally ill patients

ME Association
www.meassociation.org.uk
Information and support for those affected by ME, CFS, PVFS

Mencap
www.mencap.org.uk
Supporting people with a learning disability

Mind
www.mind.org.uk
Helps people take control of their mental health

Money Advice Service
www.moneyadviceservice.org.uk
Free, independent service to help people manage their money better

Motability
www.motability.co.uk
The national charity with overall responsibility for the Motability scheme

Motor Neurone Disease Association
www.mndassociation.org
Practical and emotional support for those affected by MND

Multiple Sclerosis Society
www.mssociety.org.uk
Information and support for those affected

Mumsnet
www.mumsnet.com
Aims to make parents' lives easier by pooling knowledge, advice and support

National Association of Funeral Directors
www.nafd.org.uk
Help in finding a funeral director

National Association of Local Councils (NALC)
www.nalc.gov.uk
Represents the interests of town and parish councils in England

National Association of Widows
www.nawidows.org.uk
Support for men and women who have lost their partners through bereavement

National Autistic Society
www.nas.org.uk
Information and support for people with autism and their families

National Council for Palliative Care
www.ncpc.org.uk
Umbrella charity for all involved in palliative, end of life and hospice care

National Debtline
www.nationaldebtline.co.uk
Free independent advice on dealing with debt problems

National Family Mediation
www.nfm.org.uk
Voluntary sector provider of family mediation

National Osteoporosis Society
www.nos.org.uk
Wide range of services to people concerned about osteoporosis

National Rail
www.nationalrail.co.uk
Information on rail travel

National Trust
www.nationaltrust.org.uk
Preserving and protecting historic places and spaces

National Will Register
www.certainty.co.uk
A national will register and search service

Natural Death Centre
www.naturaldeath.org.uk
Help, support, advice on planning a funeral

NHS Direct
www.nhsdirect.nhs.uk
Health advice online and by phone

Office of the Public Guardian
www.publicguardian.gov.uk
Supports the registration of Enduring and Lasting Powers of Attorney

Office of the Public Guardian (Scotland)
www.publicguardian-scotland.gov.uk
Supervises those appointed to manage the financial or property affairs of others

Organ Donor Register
www.organdonation.nhs.uk
How to turn good intentions about donation into action

Parkinson's UK
www.parkinsons.org.uk
Information for everyone affected by Parkinson's

Passenger Focus
www.passengerfocus.org.uk
Independent passenger watchdog

PDSA
www.pdsa.org.uk
Caring for the pets of people in need

Pensions Advisory Service
www.pensionsadvisoryservice.org.uk
Information and guidance on pensions

Pets as Therapy
www.petsastherapy.org
Provides therapeutic visits to hospitals, care homes, etc. by volunteers with dogs and cats

Pilates Foundation
www.pilatesfoundation.com
International organisation for Pilates teachers and training

Princess Royal Trust for Carers
www.carers.org
Support for carers

Ramblers Association
www.ramblers.org.uk
Promoting walking for all ages

Red Cross
www.redcross.org.uk
Helping people in crisis

Relate National Marriage Guidance
www.relate.org.uk
Country's largest provider
of relationship support

Remap
www.remap.org.uk
Helping people
with disabilities

Rethink Mental Illness
www.rethink.org
Helping people affected
by mental illness

Retired Greyhound Trust
www.retiredgreyhounds.co.uk
Finding loving homes
for greyhounds

Ricability
www.ricability.org.uk
Independent consumer research
charity providing information for
older and disabled people

**RNIB (Royal National
Institute of Blind People)**
www.rnib.org.uk
Support for blind and partially
sighted people

**SAD (Seasonal Affective
Disorder Association)**
www.sada.org.uk
Help and support for sufferers
of SAD or winter blues

Saga
www.saga.co.uk
Wide range of products and
services for the over 50s

**SAID (National Society of Allied and
Independent Funeral Directors)**
www.saif.org.uk
Help in finding a funeral director

Samaritans
www.samaritans.org.uk
Confidential emotional
support service

SANE
www.sane.org.uk
Help for anyone affected by
mental illness

Solicitors for the Elderly (SFE)
www.solicitorsfortheelderly.com
National organisation of those who
provide specialist legal advice for
older and vulnerable people

Speakability
www.speakability.org.uk
Charity supporting people
with aphasis

Specal
www.specal.co.uk
Courses, services and information
to help people with dementia

Stress Management Society
www.stress.org.uk
Helping people tackle stress

Talking Newspapers Association
www.tnauk.org.uk
Supporting blind and partially
sighted people

Telephone Preference Service
www.tpsonline.org.uk
Where to stop unwanted sales
and marketing calls

The British Tinnitus Association (BTA)
www.tinnitus.org.uk
Provides support and advice
about tinnitus

**The National Federation
of Occupational Pensioners**
www.nfop.org.uk
Campaigns to improve the
lives of members through
improved pensions

The Oldie Magazine
www.theoldie.co.uk
A splendid monthly antidote
to youth culture

The Prostate Cancer Charity
www.theprostate-cancer.org.uk
Support and information for men
affected by prostate cancer

The Relatives and Residents Association
www.relres.org
Representing the interests of older
people in residential care settings

The Right to Manage Federation
www.rtmf.org.uk
Promoting RTM and leaseholder rights

**The Scottish Partnership
for Palliative Care**
www.palliativecarescotland.org.uk
Umbrella body representing
the major organisations involved
in palliative care in Scotland

The Sequal Trust
www.thesequaltrust.org.uk
Committed to bridging the
communication gap for
disabled people of all ages

The Stroke Association
www.stroke.org.uk
Help and information for
everyone affected by stroke

Thrive
www.carryongardening.org.uk
Helping people with a disability
to start or continue gardening

Triumph Over Phobia (TOP UK)
www.topuk.org
Help for sufferers of phobia

Twitter
www.twitter.com
All the information you need
on the network

U3A. University of the Third Age
www.a3a.org.uk
Educational, creative and
leisure opportunities

Walks with Wheelchairs
www.walkswithwheelchairs.com
Information on routes suitable
for wheelchair users

Which?
www.which.co.uk
Expert, unbiased information
for consumers, whatever they
are buying

INDEX

The Oldie

Get The Oldie from just £1
Why not try Britain's funniest magazine with this special offer of 3 issues for just £1?

At a time when many magazines consist of predictable articles by predictable people, The Oldie dares to give you something different. Edited by ex-Private Eye man Richard Ingrams, it is emphatically not a magazine about retirement. We recognise that what our readers want more than anything else is good writing and amusing articles on a wide variety of topics. Does that sound like you?

Your Special Offer:

★ Get your first 3 issues for just £1 – saving £10.25 (UK, direct debit only)

★ Pay just £3.12 for future issues (saving 17%) if you decide to continue after your first 3 issues for £1

★ FREE UK delivery direct to your door

★ If you prefer to pay by credit card, no problem!

You can take 12 issues on a RISK-FREE basis for just £37.50 (saving 17%). If you change your mind, you're covered by our money-back guarantee on all un-mailed issues. Plus we'll even throw in a FREE Oldie Book of Cartoons worth £7.99. The Oldie is published every four weeks

Simply visit **www.subscribeonline.co.uk/OLD** and enter offer code HAYNES12 to place your order securely and find out more. Or call **01795 592893** today!

ORDER NOW!